WITHDRAWN

North Carolina CURIOSITIES

QUIRKY CHARACTERS, ROADSIDE ODDITIES & OTHER OFFBEAT STUFF

JON ELLISTON
AND
KENT PRIESTLEY

INSIDERS' GUIDE®

GUILFORD, CONNECTICUT
AN IMPRINT OF THE GLOBE PEQUOT PRESS

INSIDERS' GUIDE®

Copyright © 2007 by Morris Book Publishing, LLC

Text design by Nancy Freeborn
Layout by Debbie Nicolais
Maps by Rusty Nelson @ Morris Book Publishing, LLC
Photo credits p. 5 Jodi Ford, courtesy *Mountain Xpress;* p. 7 Used with permission from
The Biltmore Company, Asheville, North Carolina; p. 9 Pack Memorial Library; p. 12
Avery County Chamber of Commerce; p.21 Masato Nakagawa, Black Mountain College
Museum & Arts Center; p. 29 Donald Weiser, www.whitesquirrelart.com; p. 41, 47, 185,
187, 201, 209, 211, 215, 217, 233, 259, 265, 266, 271 North Carolina *Exploring Cultural
Heritage Online,* an LSTA supported project of the State Library of North Carolina, a divi-
sion of the Department of Cultural Resources; p. 55 Scott Lessing Hubener; p. 59
Wheels Through Time Museum; p. 73 Pisgah Astronomical Research Institute; P. 93
Michael Traister; p. 95 U.S. Army Corps of Engineers; p. 114 David Haring, Duke Lemur
Center; p. 137 Korner's Folly; p. 145 Greater Mount Airy Chamber of Commerce; p. 158
Margaret Cotrufo, North Carolina Museum of Natural Sciences; p. 174 Nation Institutes
of Health; p. 178 Preservation North Carolina; p. 220 National Institutes of Health; p.
255 Sarah S. Downing; p. 226 Elizabeth Harwick; p. 231 Roxanne Turpen; p. 237 Margie
Brooks, Hyde County Chamber of Commerce; p. 244 Cape Hattaras National Seashore;
p. 245 U.S. Geological Service; p. 247 Blaire Johnson; p. 268 U.S. Naval Air Station
Weeksville. All other photos are by the authors.

Library of Congress Cataloging-in-Publication Data is available.
ISBN: 978-0-7627-4366-7

Manufactured in the United States of America
First Edition/First Printing

Esse Quam Videri, y'all.

NORTH CAROLINA

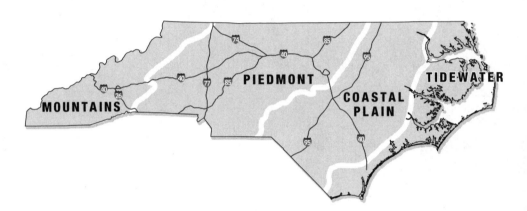

Contents

Acknowledgments

Pity the fools who try to discover curiosities on their own, without the help of their curious neighbors. We sure as heck couldn't have produced this guide to offbeat North Carolina without the generous assistance of Tar Heels all over the state.

First, a big thanks to our family members, friends, and *Mountain Xpress* co-workers (who shall remain nameless, and probably prefer it that way) for putting up with us during our mad quest. Also too numerous to name are the staff members of the visitor's bureaus, libraries, museums, and corner stores who provided anecdotes, documents, and photos that make these curiosities come alive. A special thanks to the staff of North Carolina Exploring Cultural Heritage Online, a project of the State Library of North Carolina (a division of the Department of Cultural Resources), for paying attention to and sharing so many curious details and pictures. And let's not forget those kindly folks all over who helped with directions when we lost our way.

Time to name some names, though. Thanks to: Rebecca "Bobo" Bowe," for snapping our author photo; Michael Traister, for providing the classic portrait of folk artist Clyde Jones; Sarah S. Downing of Nags Head, and Doug Stover of the National Park Service's Cape Hatteras National Seashore, for providing shipwreck photos; white squirrel photographer extraordinaire, Don Weiser (www.whitesquirrelart.com), for photos of Brevard's alabaster rodents; Margie Brooks and the Hyde County Chamber of Commerce (www.hydecounty.org) and Tom and Margie Miller and the Belhaven Community Chamber of Commerce, for valued assistance; Scott Lessing Hubener, for the curvaceous image of the Linn Cove Viaduct; Roxanne Turpen, for the shipboard shot of Sinbad; Jodi Ford and *Mountain Xpress*, for the portrait of the man who got Elvis' guitar; Henry Williams and Fred Leebron, for their literary counsel;

and Mike Urban and Gia Manalio of The Globe Pequot Press, for keeping us on track.

Then there were those who provided either free lodging during our road trips, free tips on where to find more Carolina curiosities, or both. And those who went along for the ride, for that matter. A drum roll, please, as we salute these fine folks: Phil Blank, Alvis Dunn, Brian and Fay Edwards, Matt Gocke, Catlin Hettel, Blan Holman, Kelly Lowry, Pat McCleney, April McGregor, Amy Neal, Kirk Ross, Dara Shain, Taylor Sisk, Sam Suchoff, and Alice Teich.

Preface

We recently learned that North Carolina has the greatest in-migration of any state in the Union. Which is a fancy way of saying that people are eager like never before to count themselves among the ranks of us Tar Heels.

We can't blame them, for ours is a beautiful state, brimming with industry, intellect, natural wonders, and—you'd better believe it— curiosities.

After all, the state motto is *Esse Quam Videri:* "To be, rather than to seem." In other words, what you see is what you get. We're not about putting on airs, especially when it comes to our distinctions. When we claim to be the "first in flight," we've got Orville and Wilbur Wright's famous sand dune airstrip to prove it. When we tout the world's largest Ten Commandments, we've got massive tablets to back up the claim. And when we say that Satan himself meanders around our Devil's Tramping Ground, well, you can just about smell the brimstone.

What other state can claim three stellar sets of Siamese twins that were, by turns, gentleman farmers, opera singers, and Hollywood starlets? Which can boast of harboring the world's most obsessive collectors of arrowheads, buttons, soda machines, and deviled egg plates? We've got eight-sided houses, flying saucer bachelor pads, and a mansion crammed with more than 250 rooms. And don't get us started about the state's singular festivals, which salute everything from coon dogs to sardines to men without hair.

Whether you've been here your whole life, have adopted North Carolina as your home, or are just passing through, prepare yourself for a cornucopia of wonders big and small, from the mountains to the sea. And for heaven's sake, remember to take us with you.

THE MOUNTAINS

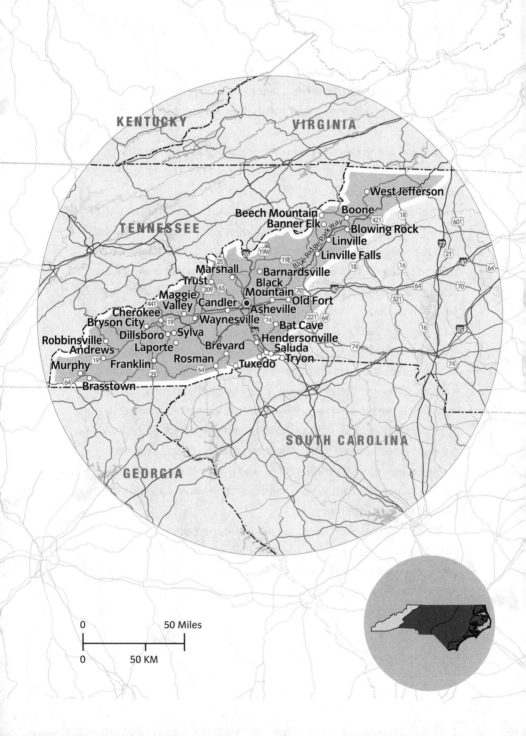

KENTUCKY

VIRGINIA

TENNESSEE

West Jefferson

Beech Mountain
Banner Elk
Boone
Blowing Rock
Linville
Linville Falls

Marshall
Barnardsville
Trust
Black
Mountain
Maggie
Valley
Candler
Asheville
Old Fort
Cherokee
Waynesville
Bat Cave
Bryson City
Dillsboro
Sylva
Hendersonville
Robbinsville
Laporte
Saluda
Andrews
Brevard
Tryon
Murphy
Franklin
Rosman
Tuxedo
Brasstown

Blue Ridge Parkway

SOUTH CAROLINA

GEORGIA

0   50 Miles

0   50 KM

THE MOUNTAINS

From time to time, some Western North Carolina wag will propose that the state's mountain region secede from Raleigh's authority and form its own state—"West Carolina" has a nice ring to it, they argue. And aside from the political motivations behind such proposals, the truth is, there *is* something different about the mountains and the people who live in them—sometimes something *mighty* different.

Need proof? Just peruse the pages of this chapter, which take you from a modern-day wagon train in Andrews to some historic church frescoes in humble West Jefferson (where they happen to celebrate Christmas in July as well as December, but that's another story). Better yet, get behind the wheel and witness the people and sights we happened upon while roaming WNC's back roads.

For starters in a little place called Suit, there's the world's largest Ten Commandments. Not far away, in Murphy, you can dig through the very Dumpster where federal fugitive Eric Rudolph got nabbed fishing for food. Then there's the world's most impressive display of aluminum Christmas trees in Brevard, which is also home to the rare (and disarmingly cute) white squirrel. And don't miss natural wonders like Sliding Rock in Pisgah Forest and the Cherokee medicine trail in Robbinsville.

If you're really ready to explore some of North Carolina's strangest phenomena, go hunting for Big Foot in Old Fort, the Brown Mountain lights in Linville Falls, or the albino bats at Moonshine Junction near Bat Cave. Whatever you find, don't say we didn't warn you. . . .

On the Wagon
Andrews

Sometimes making a political point turns out to be good fun in the end. Just ask the folks who ride the WNC Wagon Train every year.

It's one of the few—and perhaps the biggest—present-day American wagon trains. The annual event began almost fifty years ago, but it's far more than an exercise in transportation history. Instead, the organizers saddled up and took the reins as a form of equestrian protest.

People in east Tennessee and western North Carolina, you see, had a shared grievance: They didn't live far apart, geographically speaking, but often they felt worlds away, so few and poor were the roads between them. After years of fruitlessly pressing the government for a good connector highway, citizens of the two states decided in 1958 to take their gripe on the road the only way it could be done—on and behind beasts of burden.

One morning in June 1958, the first "Tellico to Murphy Wagon Train," as it was called then, left from Tellico Plains, Tennessee, and started the winding trek. The ranks of the procession swelled as people along the route joined in.

A week later, on July 4, the wagon train rolled into Murphy, where the town's streets filled with spectators, who welcomed a grand total of 67 wagons and 325 horseback riders.

Each year thereafter, some of the same folks got together and did the same thing all over again—well, almost the same thing. The wagon train has taken on different routes and destinations over the years, but every five years it follows the original Tellico-Murphy route.

And so it goes today, although new twists are always being added to what is now called the WNC Wagon Train. Each year, awards are given for best-matched horse team, most authentic covered wagon, and other superlatives. And in 2004 the organizers, who are based in

Andrews, North Carolina, added "encouragement and promotion of fair treatment of equine livestock" to their mission statement.

At the 2006 event more than one hundred people took part in the trek, which that year both started and ended in Andrews.

For all the information you need to hitch a ride next year, from registration to routes to rates, visit www.wncwagontrain.com.

Spin Control
Asheville

What did hyperactive kids do with their digits before the creation of those ubiquitous handheld video games? Well, there was Rubik's Cube in the 1980s, but think further back that that.

If you dial back a few decades, you'd find many young residents of North Carolina's mountains manipulating a marvelous little toy called the Gee Haw Whimmy Diddle. It was, in a way, a teaching tool: Using it, youngsters learned how to direct oxen and other livestock. *Gee* means "turn right"; *haw* means "turn left."

And so it goes with the Whimmy Diddle, an ingeniously simple device composed of three sticks and a nail. One straight stick is used to rub back and forth across a second, notched stick, which has a third, smaller stick attached to one end, propeller style. By holding your hands a certain way as you rub the sticks together, you can reverse the direction the propeller spins.

Of course, the first time you see it in action, the Whimmy Diddle can be puzzling. If the operators are skilled, they can just about convince you that they're reversing the spin merely through verbal commands. They'll "gee" and "haw" back and forth, and, unless you notice the subtle shift of their fingers, you're apt to think some kind of mountain magic is at work.

LAST DANCE WITH THE KING

People in almost every part of the nation can tell stories of how, at one point or another, Elvis Presley left them all shook up. But only Asheville can boast of hosting his three-day orgy of diamonds, drugs, guitars, and gunfire.

On July 22, 23, and 24, 1975, the late-edition Elvis played to sold-out crowds in the Asheville Civic Center. "He was still Elvis Presley, in all of his glory," remembers Asheville resident Nancy Fox, who took in the July 22 show as an enraptured young fan. "He was just a bigger version of Elvis."

The drama surrounding him, both onstage and off, became the stuff of Elvis legend—except these legends are true. On the downside, "bigger" Elvis had grown increasingly unstable, dogged by depression, drug abuse, and severe mood swings. In the middle of that show, Elvis unexpectedly walked off stage. Seven minutes later, he returned and said, "Ladies and gentlemen, you've heard about the king being on his throne. Well, I've been on the throne."

On the upside, Elvis still sounded great, and he was feeling extraordinarily generous. A few minutes later, he paused to tell the audience how much he loved his backup singer, gospel great J. D. Sumner, and then gave the man a $40,000, ten-carat diamond ring off his own finger.

The next day, Elvis visited a Black Mountain dentist's office, where, according to his personal doctor, George "Dr. Nick" Nichopoulos, Elvis swiped a stash of pain pills. But it was back at the Rodeway Inn, a hotel on U.S. Highway 70 just east of Asheville where Elvis's entourage occupied eighty-six rooms, that the King

The reason escapes him, but Mike Harris still has the King's guitar.

really started courting trouble. As Elvis's cronies would later explain to Charlene Noblett, then the Rodeway's general manager, Elvis got mad at the television set in his room and "shot the damn thing." (Since Elvis's death, it has been widely reported that he had something of a penchant for shooting TVs in anger.)

On his final night in Asheville, Elvis bestowed more pricey jewelry, this time on fans he seemingly chose at random. But it was twenty-one-year-old Mike Harris of Asheville who really got the kingly goods: Mid-concert, Elvis walked to the edge of the stage and gave Harris what may have been the singer's most prized guitar. It was a personalized Gibson he had commissioned back in 1968 and played in shows all over the country and in several of his movies.

After handing over the guitar, Elvis leaned down, looked Harris straight in the eye, and said, "I gave that to you for a reason."

Now, more than thirty years later, Harris admits, "I have no clue what the reason was." But he still has the guitar.

Elvis never did make it back to Asheville. He died on August 16, 1977, the day before he was to start another of his tours. It would have taken him to Asheville on August 26.

Of course, now that kids have gone digital, you might think that the Whimmy Diddle would go the way of, say, marbles or tiddlywinks. Not so, thanks to the organizers of the World Gee Haw Whimmy Diddle Competition, which is held every September. The contest has demonstrated some staying power, having been held for twenty-six years now.

The competition, long held in Oteen, is now staged at the Blue Ridge Parkway's Folk Art Center in Asheville. It has been incorporated into a weekendlong heritage festival sponsored by the Southern Highland Craft Guild that also features craft-making demonstrations, storytelling, music, and dance. For details and directions call (828) 298–7928 or visit www.southernhighlandguild.org.

Biltmore Built More
Asheville

It's no secret that George Vanderbilt's Biltmore House, built in the late 1800s, is the largest family dwelling in U.S. history. To the public's good fortune, the house and the scenic estate surrounding it have long been open to paying visitors.

And by now, you might think that you had heard all there is to hear about the 250-room mansion, which is perched on an enviable piece of property in Buncombe County. Millions of folks have visited the majestic gardens, the ornate banquet halls and boudoirs, the library bursting with books.

But in a dwelling that big, you never know what might be discovered and uncovered. Asheville's Biltmore House is a gift that keeps on giving, and it keeps revealing parts of itself.

In the spirit of full disclosure (and in the spirit of keeping a longtime tourist draw fresh, we suppose), in 2005 Biltmore House management opened up still more rooms.

Five more rooms were added to public tours: three fourth-floor maids' bedrooms, the architectural model room, and the observatory. "America's Largest Home Just Got Bigger," boasted the press release.

The Biltmore house and estate are located in the heart of Asheville's Biltmore Village. For more information call (877) 324–5866 or visit www.biltmore.com.

It took minions of maids to clean up the 250-room Biltmore House.

NEW AGE NAZI

Though few people know it today, Asheville was once home to one of the most controversial—and downright strangest—bigots to ever (dis)grace the national stage.

He found infamy here, but William Dudley Pelley was not a North Carolina native. Born in 1890 in Massachusetts, as a young man he freelanced for major magazines and wrote popular (if pulpy) novels. Then he struck gold in Hollywood, where he cranked out a series of screenplays.

But Pelley's life took a wild turn one night in 1928, when he drifted into an "ecstatic interlude," as he called it, leaving his earthly body for a mystical realm, where he purportedly made contact with deities.

Abandoning Tinseltown, Pelley moved first to New York City, where he delved into a grab bag of esoterica. In 1930 he relocated to Asheville, where he founded Galahad College, which offered classes based on Pelley's metaphysical studies.

Galahad folded after a couple of years, and in 1933 Pelley grabbed onto Adolf Hitler's coattails and founded a fascist organization he called the Silver Shirts. Chapters sprang up in twenty-two states, with the largest clusters organizing in the Midwest and on the West Coast. At its peak in the mid-1930s, Pelley's hate group numbered close to 15,000 members.

But even at their peak, the Silver Shirts remained much-ridiculed fringe dwellers. "We have seen the Silver Shirt movement for what it is," the *Asheville Times* editorialized. "In laughing at it, we laugh at others who find it a menace to the Republic."

Pelley badly jumbled his finances, and he was convicted of selling worthless stock and other financial frauds. And as the United States drifted closer to war with Nazi Germany, he steadfastly backed the Axis powers—an increasingly unpopular position.

After World War II started, Pelley was sent to federal prison on multiple charges of sedition. Paroled in 1950 he spent his remaining years in Indiana, delving further and further into the mystic. He wrote much about UFOs but little about politics. By the time of his death in 1965 at age seventy-five, he had faded into near obscurity. There were no memorials in Asheville. "He did not have a base of support here," asserts Milton Ready, a University of North Carolina–Asheville history professor. "This was just a mail drop for him."

Still, Pelley left at least small blots on history. His anti-Semitic screeds spread nationwide from his print shop, which was housed in the old Biltmore-Oteen Bank building. And several former Silver Shirts would become leaders in post–World War II fascist movements, some of them leading neo-Nazi groups well into the 1990s.

William Dudley Pelley, Asheville's flaky fascist.

A Storied Graveyard
Asheville

Oh, to be buried in Asheville.

It'd be a cool, serene resting place—and if you wound up in Riverside Cemetery, you'd have some fascinating neighbors slumbering next to you.

Deceased avid readers might enjoy the place most, for Riverside, an eighty-seven-acre cemetery roughly a mile from downtown in the Montford neighborhood, is the final resting place of two great men of letters: Thomas Wolfe (1900–1938) and O. Henry (1862–1910).

Ironically, Wolfe garnered fame largely on the basis of two novels, *Look Homeward, Angel* and the posthumously published *You Can't Go Home Again,* both of which shed a critical if thinly veiled light on his hometown of Asheville.

But when tuberculosis tackled the literary giant at a mere thirty-seven years old, his body went home from New York City to Asheville for burial at Riverside. Fittingly, his headstone bears a quote from *Look Homeward, Angel:* "The last voyage, the longest, the best."

O. Henry was the pen name of William Sydney Porter, who was born in Greensboro and became one of the country's greatest short story writers. At age forty-seven, the by-then alcoholic Porter succumbed to cirrhosis of the liver. Like Wolfe's, his body made the trip from the Big Apple to Asheville.

Other notables interred at Riverside include George Masa, the Japanese nature photographer who helped make the Blue Ridge Mountains a national treasure by documenting them on film before anyone could spoil them; James H. Posey, one of Abraham Lincoln's bodyguards; and North Carolina's Civil War governor, the iconoclastic Zebulon B. Vance.

The cemetery itself is something to behold, even for visitors who don't care much for history or literature. It is still active and so far holds more than 13,000 souls amid forested, rolling hills. There are some 9,000 monuments and twelve family mausoleums.

To get there, take the Montford exit off Interstate 240 in Asheville and follow the signs. Riverside welcomes visitors from 8:00 A.M. to 8:00 P.M. during daylight saving time, and until 6:00 P.M. the rest of the year. The cemetery's office offers self-guided tour materials. For more information, call (828) 350–2066 or visit www.ci.asheville.nc.us/parks/riverside.asp.

A Celebration of a Different Stripe

Banner Elk

A popular notion in the Appalachians holds that you can tell exactly what sort of winter weather you're in for by examining the stripes on woolly worms. And while this may or may not be scientifically verifiable, the little mountain town of Banner Elk has toasted the wooly worm and its skills at meteorological prognostication for nearly three decades. Why let "science" get in the way of a good time?

The idea for the town's annual Woolly Worm Festival came from Jim Morton, the editor of the now-defunct magazine *Mountain Living,* back in the late 1970s. One day, Morton got his hands on a woolly worm caterpillar (the larva of the common Isabella tiger moth) and deduced the winter forecast from it for use in his magazine. Things were fine until the next day, when Morton ran across another wooly worm with completely different markings.

The wisdom Morton gleaned from this experience is that only one worm can be consulted per year. So, since 1978, Banner Elk has set aside the third weekend in October as the time to decide which woolly worm will win the right to predict the severity of the coming winter. Worms do this not by arm-wrestling or broad-jumping but by racing up a 3-foot length of string.

Woolly worm caterpillars (also called woolly bears) are marked with thirteen segments, alternating light and dark. Tradition has it that the segments correspond to the thirteen weeks of winter. By this logic, the lighter brown a particular segment is, the milder that week will be. The darker it is, well, Katy, bar the door: You're in for some snow and serious cold.

Winter is big business in Avery County. The state's two largest ski resorts—Beech Mountain and Wolf Laurel—are close by, so it stands to reason that the winning worm's markings are of no small import.

About 20,000 people attend the festival each year, many bringing their own worms with them. The competitors have clever names. Past entrants, for instance, have included Patsy Climb and Dale Wormhardt. (Lean close and you may hear the losing worms whisper, "I coulda been a contender!")

Saturday's proceedings include a solid day of races, twenty worms at a go, until a final race takes place around 4:00 P.M. The winning worm gets official weather-worm status; its owner makes out considerably better, taking home $1,000. Informal races—for the love of the sport—continue on Sunday.

Banner Elk's Woolly Worm Festival also features crafts, food vendors, live entertainment, and more. Organizers include the Avery Banner Elk

Woolly Worm Festival. All this for a two-inch, squirming larva.

Chamber of Commerce and the Kiwanis Club of Banner Elk. A portion of the proceeds goes to support children's charities throughout Avery County. For more information, call (828) 898–5605.

Banner Elk is located at the junction of Highways 194 and 184 in Avery County.

UFO A-Go-Go
Barnardsville

"The truth is out there," or so the saying goes. If you think *you're* never going to see a UFO, Joshua Warren has a way to convince you otherwise. Show up at his annual UFO Experience, and you're guaranteed to see several.

It bears mentioning that they happen to be fakes—which is to say that, so far at least, the strange craft that fill a corner of the Barnardsville sky are created by terrestrials using decidedly earthly items like helium-filled balloons and light sticks.

Warren, who heads the Asheville-based paranormal research team LEMUR, has written widely about unexplained phenomena and hosts a weekly radio talk show, *Speaking of Strange.* In 2005 he organized the first UFO Experience and invited the public to come share in his fascination.

"This event serves two purposes," he explained. "Seeing creative, fake UFOs will help us rule out fakes when analyzing UFO pictures and footage. Secondly, it's just going to be downright fun."

And so it is: Late on a weekend afternoon in August, participants gather at the Barnardsville Community Center for a potluck-style cookout. After sunset, the homemade UFOs are hoisted, one by one, into the night sky. The creator of the craft judged the best receives a prize package.

"If you haven't seen an actual UFO," Warren says, "this should at least give you the experience to some degree." Maybe, maybe not. But either way, it's a close encounter with some fun-loving UFO buffs.

The UFO Experience is free and open to the public, but donations to cover the rent of the event space are appreciated, and it's best to bring your own food and UFO-construction materials. And, oh yeah, don't forget to bring something to tether your craft with—we wouldn't want that fake UFO to wander off and spark a spate of sightings, would we?

For details on next year's UFO Experience, visit www.speakingof strange.com.

How's It Hanging?

Bat Cave

The cove forest that surrounds Bat Cave is verdant and thick with rare plants like Carey's saxifrage and broadleaf coreopsis. Natural vents wheeze air from the bowels of the earth, cool and moist. Deep underground, little-known creatures—spiders, crevice salamanders, millipedes, amphipods—skulk about, only too happy to be left in the dark. And then, of course, there are those bats, all papery wings and pug noses. Cute!

In 1981 The Nature Conservancy assumed management of the delicate Henderson County preserve, which today is co-owned by the organization and Margaret Flinsch. And while it remains off-limits to visitation most of the year, in summer the curious can set foot on the 186-acre parcel during weekly tours.

Each year, The Nature Conservancy trains students from Warren Wilson College in nearby Swannanoa to help steward the preserve. Stewards lead the hikes of the property, which stop short of the cave entrance. There's no guarantee you'll see a bat ("They're mostly sleeping during the day," The Nature Conservancy's Maria Sadowski admits), but the views from the trail and the plant diversity promise to make the trip worthwhile.

The tours are in support of the organization's goals at the preserve, which include reestablishing the endangered Indiana bat, a formerly common denizen of the cave. Rare flora and fauna are not the only distinction: With its 300-foot-long and 85-foot-high main chamber, Bat Cave ranks as North America's largest granite fissure cave. Now you know what all the flap is about.

The Bat Cave Preserve tours are $10.00 for adults and $5.00 for children under twelve. Hikes require preregistration, and space is limited. Call The Nature Conservatory's Mountain office at (828) 749–1700 to sign up. Bat Cave is located 22 miles south of Asheville on U.S. Highway 64. Visitors eager to bring home a souvenir will find no shortage of bat-themed bumper stickers, license plates, pens, T-shirts, and more in local shops, lodges, and restaurants.

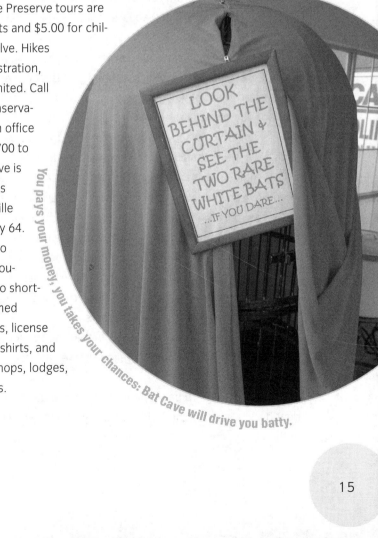

You pays your money, you takes your chances: Bat Cave will drive you batty.

15

Moonshine Junction
Bat Cave

Tourists, don't let the name throw you—Moonshine Junction is not some kind of mountain speakeasy serving illicit corn liquor. "Everyone wants to know if we sell moonshine," says Richard Tedesco, who co-owns the store with his wife, Linda. "I don't think they realize that it's illegal."

Instead of 'shine, there's plenty of legal—if quite strange—fun to be had at this souvenir, craft, and curio store tucked into the curvy, tree-lined road that runs from Lake Lure to Asheville and back. Roaming Moonshine Junction's 4,000-square-foot space, you never know what you'll encounter next.

There are the mainstays of the region's roadside shops: Appalachian antiques, quilts, jewelry, knives, canned goods, and the like. There's also a good share of gag gifts, from old-fashioned peashooters to modern-day spray cans of fake poop.

The longer you wander around the place, the weirder it gets. On one shelf a giant frog is suspended in formaldehyde. (His last swim?) On a wall a vintage soapbox derby racer sets emblazoned with the Kentucky Fried Chicken logo and good ol' Colonel Sanders. (DO NOT TOUCH. REALLY. THIS MEANS YOU, a sign reads.) In the next room there's an old-timey ice-cream shop—normal enough, until you notice the nearby glass tank with "two baby rattlers" nestled among the rocks.

But you ain't seen nothin' yet. Around the corner sits Moonshine Junction's premier attraction: a curtained cage with a sign bearing the words SEE TWO RARE WHITE BATS—IF YOU DARE.

Well, we dared, and what we saw in that cage cannot be described here—you really must see it to believe it. We can offer some advice, however: Brace yourself.

Likewise, it pays to be prepared to meet Cletus, the Junction's resident hillbilly. Just ask the Tedescos nicely, and they can usually arrange for him to appear.

And while you can have scads of fun simply exploring Moonshine Junction, don't forget that it's a store, after all. "Most of the people who come in here say, 'Wow, you have a lot of stuff, a little bit of something for everyone'—and they usually are the people who don't buy anything,"

Dentists see dollar signs when they meet Richard and Linda Tedesco.

Richard deadpans. "I like the people who don't like my store and spend lots of money more than the people who love my store and don't buy anything."

Moonshine Junction is located on U.S. Highway 74-A about 7 miles from Lake Lure and 20 miles from Asheville. From either direction, you can't miss it. The store is open from 10:00 A.M. to 5:00 P.M. daily, except for Tuesday and Wednesday (and hours are sometimes reduced in the winter months). Find out more at www.moonshinejunction.com or by calling (828) 625–1535.

Not in Kansas Anymore
Beech Mountain

Pity the former theme park. The gates are closed; the lights are off. Where children's excited voices once echoed, there's only silence. In most cases, the property is sold off, the rides and exhibits are torn down or go to auction, and, over time, all vestiges of the park fade away.

Not so at the Land of Oz, a once-popular theme park that opened in 1970 and drew 400,000 visitors in its first year. Ten years later, attendance had waned to the point that the park closed.

The park had a good run, judging by the memories that are conjured up by the thousands of people who still speak fondly of the Land of Oz today. Its chief attribute, many say, was the sheer authenticity of it all—the sixteen-acre park was complete with replicas of Uncle Henry's farm and Emerald City, costumed performers of all the major characters from the movie, and—you guessed it—long stretches of yellow brick road.

Today, the land that was Oz sits inside a sizable housing development called, appropriately enough, Emerald Mountain ("There's no place like home," residents have been heard to say). So it's all on private property—but Oz fans, take courage (as the Cowardly Lion would say): Once a year, the public gets a chance to walk in Dorothy's red shoes. The first weekend in October, locals stage a two-day "Autumn of Oz" party, inviting visitors to take a "nostalgic stroll" through what once were the theme park grounds for a nominal fee.

For more information, call Emerald Mountain at (828) 387–2000 or visit www.emeraldmtn.com (the site offers complete directions from all directions).

Gravity Goes Missing
Blowing Rock

They come from far and wide to visit Mystery Hill. And who can blame them? Where else can you watch a ball roll uphill or see your friends and family pulled from an upright stance to something approaching a 45-degree angle? It's just the sort of thing every teenager prays will happen to his kid brother, and it's been happening for generations at this Blowing Rock wayside.

The gravity-free zone is located at the appropriately named Mystery House. If that's not mystery enough, nearby, the Hall of Mystery is chock-full of stumpers, experiments, and optical illusions, including a Bubble-Rama, a Spooky Spigot, a Magic Lightbulb, and the Flying Mirror (Duck!).

We won't reveal more here, because we are of the firm belief that mysteries should remain thus. But suffice it to say, the folks at Mystery Hill are mighty friendly, and what's more, their gravity-defying attraction also includes the fabulous arrowhead and Indian pottery collection of the late "Moon" Mullins, who, with his wife, Marion, collected some 50,000 of the sharpened stones over the years.

For more information, call (828) 264–2792 or visit www.mystery hill-nc.com. Mystery Hill is located at 129 Mystery Hill Lane near Blowing Rock, just off U.S. Highway 321.

HOME OF THE DOME

Structure, science, and style. The three came together in Black Mountain, where visionary thinker and doer R. Buckminster Fuller (1895–1983) built the first of his geodesic domes. The futuristic structure was a milestone in what might be called humanistic design.

Lloyd Sieden described how "Bucky" did it in a 1989 article in the journal *The Futurist*. When Fuller set out to craft the perfect dome, using the principles of spherical geometry, he was trying to find "nature's coordinate system" and build "a structure that would, because it was based on natural rather than humanly developed principles, be extremely efficient," Sieden wrote. The construction he created was the geodesic dome, which, Sieden noted, "encloses much more space with far less material than conventional buildings."

The unconventional project required an unconventional space in which to build it. So in the summer of 1948, Fuller took his head full of dome dreams to Black Mountain College, an avant-garde institution that was a hotbed of artistic and cultural innovation.

Fuller had previously worked in architecture and construction, fields that deeply shaped his thinking. "He came to realize that the dome pattern had been employed, to some extent, ever since humans began building structures," Sieden noted. "Early sailors landing upon foreign shores and requiring immediate shelter would simply upend their ships, creating an arched shelter similar to a dome."

With help from the college's students and some fellow instructors, Fuller spent much of the summer designing a new sort of dome. He acquired a sizable store of Venetian blind strips, his basic building

Bucky Fuller's 1949 dome. Bucky and friends, kickin' it geodesic style.

CONTINUED

materials. By September the prototype design was complete, and Fuller and crew erected the first geodesic dome.

That first dome was an impressive but short-lived structure—within moments of going up, it sagged from its own weight and crumpled to the ground.

So Fuller spent another year back at the drawing board, trying to get the spines of the dome in perfect position. In the summer of 1949, he returned to Black Mountain College to give it another go. With help from students from the Chicago Institute of Design, this time the inventor pulled it off. Built with aluminum aircraft tubing, his second dome, which was 14 feet in diameter, stood strong. He covered it in vinyl, and—voilà—a lightweight and functional structure was born.

Fuller went on to craft domes of many sizes, from all sorts of building materials, and today the geodesic wonders can be found in dozens of countries and serving as everything from housing to concert arenas to "immersive environments"—wherein multimedia artists and educators use the dome's ceiling and walls as a canvas for creating virtual realities. Perhaps the most recognizable one in the United States is "Spaceship Earth," a main attraction at the EPCOT Center at Disney World in Orlando, which has a diameter of 165 feet and houses an educational amusement ride.

Today, the Black Mountain College legacy is kept alive by Asheville's Black Mountain College Museum + Arts Center, which hosts regular exhibits of work by Fuller and his academic colleagues. For information on the latest programs and hours, visit www.blackmountaincollege.org.

Into the Wild
Boone

Eustace Conway's list of achievements in the natural world is singular. Years ago he hiked the Appalachian Trail, one-upping his fellow through-hikers by subsisting largely on food he found along the way; later, he kayaked the length of the southern Alaskan coast; he back-packed through 5,000 miles of wilderness on four continents besides North America; he canoed the majority of the Mississippi; he set a coast-to-coast on-horseback record, traveling from the Pacific to the Atlantic in a short 103-day span. Through most of the same period—when not venturing out—Conway lived in a tepee. Simply put, Conway is unlike most of his contemporaries, many of whom have trouble surviving a single day without a latte and a clean pair of boxer briefs.

Today, Conway, with a ready smile and a growth of frizzled beard, runs Turtle Island Preserve, a camp near Boone. Visitors to Turtle Island can help Conway plant and harvest in the preserve's generous gardens, learn how to milk goats, and learn the means to make a variety of things that make life in the wilds easier: spoons, bowls, tools, butter, soap. A visit to the preserve is conceived as a "total cultural experience," removing people from the everyday grind and immersing them in a lifestyle where their own skills and capabilities intersect with nature's abundance, a state that—it is hoped—inspires awe and renewed appreciation of the natural world.

To get your own taste of Conway's vision, visit www.turtleisland preserve.com or call (828) 265–2267. The preserve's gravel road begins at 443 Lonnie Carlton Road in Triplett.

A Real Letdown

Brasstown

The opossum has been a fixture of southern life and lore since time out of mind—even heralded in song ("Possum is a pretty thing, he rambles in the dark, only time you know he's 'round is when you hear old Ranger bark")—so it's natural that the little burg of Brasstown rings in the New Year by lowering a caged one from a gas station roof.

Wait. Did we just say that? Yes, we did. New York City has its Waterford crystal ball; Atlanta has its giant peach. Brasstown has its nocturnal marsupial in a Plexiglas cage. The annual turn-of-the-year event is called the Possum Drop, and it's the brainchild of a fellow named Clay Logan, owner of Clay's Corner, a store and Citgo station that might be the world's best-stocked purveyor of possum memorabilia.

The Possum Drop draws hundreds each year, swelling Brasstown's usual population of 240 as much as threefold. In 2004 it also drew the attention of PETA, the nation's best-known animal-rights organization. With PETA breathing down his neck, Logan had to find a roadkill possum in a pinch or suffer a media smear campaign from the group. Logan prevailed (possums have a knack for wandering into traffic), but Brasstowners were unified in their agreement that the dead-possum event was lame compared to those of years past.

Since then, event organizers have returned to using a live possum, with the assurance that it's treated with the utmost care and respect (not to mention returned to the wilds unscathed). Surely such treatment is nothing less than such a "pretty thing" deserves.

Clay's Corner is located at 11005 Old Highway 64 West in Brasstown. Call (828) 837–3797 or visit www.clayscorner.com.

Aluminum Tree and Ornament Museum

Brevard

Snicker, snicker. How tacky! Oh heck, I've got to get me one.

That's a common reaction to a room full of aluminum Christmas trees, those delightfully kitschy relics of the modern holiday season. Seems that real, green trees didn't cut it for some people. So, shirking tradition, they went aluminum—and set off a short-lived consumer craze for the faux firs that ran from the 1950s through the 1970s.

Stephan Jackson, a home designer in Brevard, was bitten by the aluminum tree bug in 1991, when he received his first one as a gift. Mining flea markets and yard sales, he started building a collection of them, which today stands at more than sixty vintage trees (and he's got thousands of tacky ornaments to hang on them, to boot).

Tongue firmly in cheek, Jackson gave his collection an appropriately space-age name: ATOM, a strained acronym for the museum's full name (the Aluminum Tree and Aesthetically Challenged Seasonal Ornament Museum and Research Center). He didn't want to keep all that metallic brilliance to himself, so he began unveiling them for the public as a rotating annual exhibit. For some holiday seasons it's held in Brevard. For others it's in Asheville or other nearby towns.

For the latest news on ATOM's exhibits, visit www.aluminumtree.com.

Kitsch as kitsch can: At the aluminum Christmas tree museum, no ornament is off-limits.

Tall in the Saddle

Brevard

Jim Bob Tinsley—craftsman, cowboy crooner, sportsman nonpareil, naturalist, polymath, antiquarian, and lover of the wide-open spaces—was one of those rare people who always seem to be at the right place at the right time.

Tinsley died in 2004, but his complex legacy, not to mention a bunch of his stuff, lives on at the museum named after him in Brevard.

Born here in 1921, Tinsley became enraptured by western music in his teens. He eventually headed up a musical group that broadcast from Asheville, and later he toured the United States with Gene Autry for a spell.

Called into service during World War II, Tinsley spent four years as an aerial photographer. In 1943, during duty in Casablanca, he crossed paths with Allied leader Winston Churchill. Tinsley was sitting on a barracks' steps strumming tunes with friends when a limousine pulled up.

Thomas Frederickson is happy to be saddled with the job of museum treasurer.

"Can you play 'You Are My Sunshine'?" asked a jowly Englishman within. Tinsley said he could, and what followed was a brief world summit of song.

In 1949 Tinsley married his wife, Dottie, and the couple honeymooned in Florida, where Tinsley went Gulf Stream fishing and set the one-day record for number of sailfish caught. One of his stuffed catches hangs from the museum's wall; nearby is a sailfish pennant flown from the boat that day as well as a picture of Tinsley in the fighting chair.

Inspired by his catch, Tinsley—according to the museum's displays—went on to write the first definitive book on the sailfish and, later, a "hemispheric study" of the puma, or mountain lion, another game animal he had a knack for bagging.

Later in life, he focused most of his attention and pride on the waterfalls of his native Transylvania County. Through it all, he and Dottie saved a lot of interesting things.

"He and his wife didn't throw anything away," says Thomas Frederickson, the museum's self-described "docent, maintenance man, treasurer, general factotum."

"It turned out nice for us that they did keep all this stuff because now we have all of it on display," Frederickson adds. That "stuff" includes a centuries-old Gillespie rifle, a collection of western saddles, and a fluoroscope—a novelty X-ray machine that was once common in shoe stores. There are Indian blankets, cowboy portraits, and a huge, carved chair made by Tinsley.

Standing watch over all this is a TV in the corner, which loops a video of Jim Bob leading a sing-along, his warm voice as big and clear as the high plains: "Tumblin' along with the tumblin' tumbleweeds." Tumble on, Jim Bob.

The museum is located at 20 West Jordan Street in Brevard. Call (828) 884–2347 or visit www.jimbobtinsleymuseum.org for hours and additional information.

Rodents Gone Wild
Brevard

What's white, bucktoothed, and loves to climb trees? No, silly, it's not that nephew of yours. Why, it's the white squirrels of Brevard, of course!

Iconic animals are a vital part of American city life. Think, if you will, of San Juan Capistrano and its swallows, Portland and its lobsters, Miami and its roaches. Apparently it wasn't enough for Brevard, North Carolina, to have the nation's largest concentration of natural waterfalls nearby. The place needed, well, something different.

It got it in the form of squirrels. According to local legend, North Carolina's favorite pale rodents first appeared in Brevard in the 1940s in the care of Mr. H. H. Mull. Evidently, a Mr. Black of Madison, Florida, gave Mull a pair of the squirrels not long after finding them playing in his pecan grove. (An overturned carnival truck was the original source.)

Mull in turn gave them to his daughter, who kept the squirrels in a cage in hopes of breeding them. As fate would have it, though, the animals were unable—think of pandas or prisoners—to breed in captivity. Then, in 1951, Mull's daughter left home, and one of the squirrels escaped. So what did Mull do? He let the other one go. Soon, people began spotting white squirrels in locations all over town. The squirrels' lovemaking had apparently gathered some steam once they returned to the wild.

The rest, as they say, is history.

The animals became such a badge of distinction that in 1986 the Brevard City Council voted unanimously to pass an ordinance protecting them. It states:

"The entire area embraced within the corporate limits of the city is hereby designated as a sanctuary for all species of squirrel (family *Sciuriadae*), and in particular the 'Brevard White Squirrel.' It shall be unlawful for any person to hunt, kill, trap, or otherwise take protected squirrels within the city."

It might be tempting to pass off Brevard's white squirrels as albinos, a rare (1 in 17,000) incidence in which animals lack melanin, the pigment that gives skin its color. With albinism animals' eyes tend to be pink. But the Brevard squirrels, it turns out, have normal, black eyes. They are not a distinct breed, either; they can interbreed with the common gray squirrels that inhabited Brevard long before Mull's daughter roamed this earth.

Don't call me "albino," pal — I'm one of Brevard's white squirrels.

For the past several years the town has hosted a White Squirrel Festival at the end of May. Along with musical acts, vendors, and craft demonstrations, the festival includes walking tours to see real white squirrels, a White Squirrel Children's Village, and a white squirrel photo op. For information, call Heart of Brevard at (828) 884–3278 or visit www.brevardnc.org. Brevard is located at the junction of U.S. Highways 64 and 276 in Transylvania County.

Slippery When Wet
Brevard

The North Carolina mountains suffer no shortage of waterfalls, cascading river drops that churn out perpetual awe and inspiration. Many are located within easy striking distance of state highways or the Blue Ridge Parkway. But none are as tailor-made for fun as Sliding Rock, a 60-foot natural waterslide located in the Pisgah National Forest near Brevard.

The rock in question rises up above an 8-foot-deep pool at its base, much like a massive, concerned forehead. Visitors can thread their way up the rock with the help of a handrail, then slide, plunge, and walk up to do it all over again.

On average, 11,000 gallons of water pass down the rock each hour. Its water stays a bracing 50 to 60 degrees even on the hottest days.

A summer weekend at Sliding Rock is nearly as much fun for watchers as it is for sliders. A wooden observation platform across from the falls gives full view of the human throng—in all shapes, sizes, and degrees of fitness—that goes down it in the course of a day.

Sliding Rock has been groomed into a recreation area by the U.S. Forest Service. In the interest of safe sliding, lifeguards are on duty from Memorial Day through Labor Day. Visits are permitted any day of the year, but those who slide off-season do so at their own risk (and at risk of hypothermia). Nearby bathrooms and changing rooms are also open in-season. A nominal fee is charged to enter the Sliding Rock recreation area ($3.00 per car at the time of printing).

Water comes and water goes, but Sliding Rock abides. Likely it will always be one of the state's favorite places to wear out the seat of one's pants.

To get there, travel from north from Pisgah Forest on US 276 for about 8 miles. After you've gone 5 miles, you'll pass Looking Glass Falls on the right. Look for signs directing you to the Sliding Rock recreation area parking lot on the left. For the slider who can't get enough, the nearest camping is at the Forest Service's Davidson River Campground.

For more information, contact the National Forest Service's Pisgah National Forest office at (828) 877–3350. To learn more about nearby recreation and camping opportunities, visit www.cs.unca.edu/nfsnc.

The Road Less Traveled
Bryson City

Seven miles west of Bryson City, Highway 288, a meandering, two-lane road, ends abruptly at a screen of woods. Locals call it "The Road to Nowhere."

The road was intended to cross the southern portion of the Great Smoky Mountains National Park and connect western North Carolina to Tennessee, but it never got that far. Construction began in the 1960s but was halted a decade later because of cost and environmental concerns. A few steep portions of the road collapsed in landslides, and studies revealed that the soils the road was being built on were leaching acid into several of the pristine trout streams the highway crossed.

Still, a lot of locals around Bryson City and elsewhere in Swain

County are hopping mad about the fact that the road has never been finished. A good number of their ancestors—roughly 600 families—were displaced from the area in the 1940s, when the Tennessee River Valley was flooded to create Lake Fontana, a hydroelectric reservoir needed for wartime power production. Some of their families' crumbling homesteads still stand along the north shore of the lake, and several family cemeteries rise amid the woods, too.

"Our folks were promised this road, and we haven't gotten it," says David Monteith, whose family was one of those removed from the Tennessee Valley during the war.

But times change, and costs projected for the road during the original flurry of construction are astronomically higher today, given inflation and the expense of environmental mitigation. Building the road now, it is projected, would cost in excess of $590 million.

Still, supporters like Monteith balk at arguments that finishing the road would be too costly. "Cost is not the issue," he said. "Principle is the issue. Those people gave all they had."

Some politicians have promised that funding for the road will become available; others have suggested that the federal government settle with Swain County for the cost of the road. However the story ends—road or no road—in Swain County, at least, it would be hard to overestimate the power of a broken promise.

To reach "The Road to Nowhere," take Highway 19 west to Bryson City. Turn right onto Everett Street; continue on Everett until it becomes Fontana Road (Road to Nowhere).

WHAT'S IN A NAME?

The proud people of Buncombe County aren't "insincere," and they don't speak "foolish nonsense." But by a quirky twist of etymology, the county's moniker has come to mean something along those not-so-flattering lines.

To understand how this came to be, we must travel back in time to 1820 and meet Congressman Felix Walker of Buncombe County. In the midst of a particularly tedious debate about the Missouri Compromise in the U.S. House of Representatives, Walker took to the podium and delivered a rambling discourse about, well, nothing in particular (or at least nothing anyone could remember thereafter).

Walker's congressional colleagues were having none of it. They fidgeted, rolled their eyes, and collectively sighed. Still, Walker droned on.

After his marathon monologue was complete, a group of congressmen implored him to explain why he had blathered on so. Well, he answered, he figured that it was his job "to make a speech for Buncombe."

And so the pejorative phonetic was born. Before long, Washington's political set was using the term bunkum to describe empty, meaningless speech. Over time, the word spread nationwide and has also seen much use in the short form—bunk.

But lest anyone think that the good people of Buncombe County have nothing meaningful to say, just try them—they'd be more than happy to debunk the notion.

Toot, Toot
Bryson City

There are model train museums, and then there are model train museums. Smoky Mountain Trains is one that runs full bore.

Home to more than 7,000 Lionel company engines, cars, and accessories, the collection that rides the rails here dates back to the early 1900s and covers all the ground since then. At any given time, at least six model trains are running on what together amounts to more than 1 mile of model track. Some of them pass through a replica roundhouse, and others under a real 5-foot waterfall.

You'd be hard-pressed to find a place where tiny trains travel in finer fashion. Smoky Mountain Trains is located at 100 Greenlee Street, next to the Great Smoky Mountains Railroad Depot, and is open from 8:30 A.M. to 5:30 P.M., Monday through Saturday. Call (866) 914–5200 or visit www.smokymtntrains.com.

The Garlic Freak
Candler

The "stinking rose" may have its origins in Siberia, but apparently it's quite content in the Appalachian coves near Candler, North Carolina. Tom Sherry grows forty varieties of garlic at his Whistlepig Farm, twenty minutes west of Asheville. He calls himself a "garlic freak" and, to prove it, a few years ago seized the domain name on the Internet to help him market the pungent vegetable from his cozy seven-acre farm.

Outside of certain gustatory circles, most people know of only one kind of garlic, the soft-neck style grown in California's Central Valley, with its elaborate ruffle of papery skins cloaking each clove. But there are possibly hundreds of varieties of garlic around the world—hard necks, soft necks, turbans, artichokes, porcelains, Creoles, rocamboles.

Some have colorful wrappers, satiny wrappers, or pearlescent wrappers. Others are marked with stripes or red tips. Their flavors are equally varied—allowing for the classic garlic pungency—and run from mild to fiery. Their names—Persian Star, Wild Buff, Polish Hardneck Glazer, Lotus, Tzan, Pskem, Oregon Blue, Asian Tempest—suggest a world of flavor.

In fact, Sherry might be more than just a farmer with a quirky passion. He may be a visionary in dirt-stained Carhartt overalls.

"Garlic Freak" Tom Sherry is ready to take on an army of vampires.

"People say, 'It's just garlic.' And I tell them, yeah, well in 1980, coffee was 'just coffee' and in 1990 beer was 'just beer.' In 2006 garlic is still just garlic. But go to a supermarket now and there are 45 different kinds of coffee and 150 kinds of beer. It could be the same for garlic one day. We're at the front end of that curve."

Garlic originated in Siberia and moved west with the spice trade. Sherry's movements have been less exotic: He grew up in Pennsylvania but has lived most of his adult life in North Carolina. Several years ago he was tending a bed of garlic plants when he fell in love.

"The hard-neck garlics, in the spring, send up this little scape," he says, describing the elegant, spiraling bud that emerges from the plants. "And I didn't know anything about them. But right then I was like, 'That's it. It's over. I'm sold.'"

A half decade later, he's no less enamored of the plant, which he insists defies categorization.

"Garlic doesn't fit into any real food category. It's not considered a vegetable, it's not considered a spice, it's not considered an herb. If you think about it, it exists in its own little universe."

Unlike most farm crops, garlic grows through the winter. Sherry plants in mid-fall and harvests in June. Then he hangs the plants to dry, grades them for the choicest bulbs, and packs them in boxes for sale as garlic samplers.

Sherry's Whistlepig Farm garlic assortment may never have the selling power of, say, a Whitman sampler, but he nevertheless manages to sell out every season, a sign that his gospel of garlic may have roots after all.

"People don't freak out over kale," he says, smiling. "They don't freak out over cauliflower. They *do* freak out over garlic. People get a rush over certain food items, and garlic is one of those. With good garlic you can make someone smile."

To get your own taste of Whistlepig Farm garlic, visit www.garlic freak.com.

Are You Tough Enough?

Cherokee

The anthropologist James Mooney, who lived among the Cherokee in the 1880s, gave this view of the hands-off, everything-goes tribal sport known as stickball: "Almost everything short of murder is allowable in the game, and both parties sometimes go into the contest with the deliberate purpose of crippling or otherwise disabling the best players on the opposing side. Serious accidents are common."

This is one fierce game we're talking about. Stickball, in rough outline, is similar to lacrosse, which the Canadian settlers adapted from the Algonquian tribes who lived there. Players carry racquets of bent wood fitted with a woven pouch at one end (the "sticks" that give the game its name). Using these racquets they throw a small hide ball down a large playing field. A team scores a point when a player throws the ball between two vertical posts at the end of the field or touches one of the posts with the ball. Typically the game is played to twelve points.

Stickball was, and remains, rough. The Cherokee called it "the little war," and historically matches were played between rival towns. It was also used as a way to settle scores. Games could last as long as two days, with enough split shins and broken bones to make contemporary NFL players cower and cry "mommy."

In former times stickball players were so serious about the sport that they stuck to an elaborate pregame ritual, which involved abstaining from rabbit meat (a tribal favorite), because rabbits were seen as timid and easily confused, qualities that might transfer to the eater. "Above all," wrote Mooney, a player "must not touch a woman, and the player who should violate this regulation would expose himself to the summary vengeance of his fellows." Players also scratched fearsome designs on their bare flesh with charcoal.

It's not a spectator sport for the faint of heart, but stickball is still played on the Cherokee Reservation in exhibitions, including the tribe's fall festival. For information about the sport and match times, call (800) 438–1601 or visit www.cherokee-nc.com.

Easter Hat Parade
Dillsboro

Hats off to you, Dillsboro, for unabashedly donning your bonnets. Maybe it takes a tiny town to make a big deal about an annual parade that draws only a few hundred people. But it definitely takes a big holiday spirit—and a willingness to laugh at both your neighbors and yourself—to pull off the Easter Hat Parade the way Dillsboro does.

The event might better be called "Anything You Can Put on Your Head Day." Ever since 1988, on the Saturday before Easter, the town has rallied in perfect municipal-parade fashion. The parade is led by a local fire truck, which is followed by a procession of classic cars driven by Waynesville's Mountaineer Antique Automotive Club and, finally, the hat-wearing revelers—who range from toddlers to grannies to pets. After a march around town, awards are dispensed for the most superlative hats—the biggest, the smallest, the most historical, the best-smelling, the poofiest, and so on.

(And just in case you make it to the parade without a hat of your own, don't worry: There's a wide assortment on hand that can be rented on the cheap.)

There's some order and some disorder, and, by the end, everyone's seen enough hats festooned with flowers, eggs, various forms of plant life, figurines, and curios of every sort to go home knowing they've seen something they won't see anywhere else.

For information on next year's Easter Hat Parade, visit the Dillsboro Merchants' Association Web site at www.visitdillsboro.org.

In their Easter bonnets, with all the . . . upon it.

Don't He Look Natural?

Franklin

Put aside those images of Norman Bates. Taxidermy, when practiced by sane people, is a skilled and highly regarded art form. Not just anyone can schlep a skin, mount it on a foam or plastic form, and expect the results to give the impression of life.

Bill and Linda Fuchs have a knack for the taxidermist's art; in fact, they've got more than four decades of experience preserving, restoring, and raising the dead. They've won a slew of state, national, and international awards for their work, and, lucky for us, a while back they decided to put a good portion of it on display. The result, the Wilderness Taxidermy & Outfitters museum, is a 6,000-square-foot collection of the marvels of the stuffed world. See the world's third-largest lion! See man-eating crocodiles! See winged and finned specimens, from the lowly barnyard rooster to swordfish and pompano! All of them look good, and none of them, presumably, will try to bite or spur you.

Many of the animals are posed in lifelike settings, including a black bear with a mouthful of salmon, mountain goats toeing a craggy alpine shelf, and a lion tearing the haunches off an antelope. It simply doesn't get better than this.

What's more, the Fuchses' workshop is located here. If you've got a skin for the stuffing—a meddlesome groundhog, perhaps, or a trophy bass, or the neighbor's kid whom grandpa backed over in his Lincoln (kidding!)—call ahead for the price of getting it mounted, right down to "museum-quality eyes."

Wilderness Taxidermy Inc. is located at 5040 Highlands Road in Franklin, a little ways off US 64. Call (828) 524–3677 or visit www .wildernesstaxidermy.com for more information.

THE MOUNTAINS

What Doesn't Kilt Me Makes Me Stronger
Franklin

The settlers of North Carolina's mountains were known for their fierceness and independence, their affection for making illicit liquor, and their indignation in the face of government meddling. Those traits had an antecedent: Almost to a family, the first wave of would-be mountain people who reached these green hills were from Scotland or Scots-settled plantations in Northern Ireland, places that had known centuries of squabbling and clan-on-clan violence.

The authors of this book both have Scots blood way up in them, but no, sir, you won't find us trotting around in kilts (at least not yet). Still, the popularity of Scottish games at places like Grandfather Mountain shows that a lot of North Carolinians wear their heritage as proud as can be, even if it means wearing a skirt, for Pete's sake.

Franklin's Scottish Tartan Museum opened in 1988 as a way of celebrating the region's Scottish heritage and displaying the origins and evolution of tartans, the plaid patterns specific to different clans or families; and the kilt, the Scottish man's traditional garb. Along with the hundreds of swatches of tartan that line the walls and a working loom, Scottish history is on display here in miniature, as well as a

There are some great Scots under these kilts.

41

collection of Scottish weapons and information about the early settlers' interactions with the Cherokee, the original owners of these mountains. The museum is an ample 4,800 square feet and attracts about 15,000 visitors a year.

If a visit simply isn't enough, the museum staff will help you order a tartan or kilt of your own. The gift store sells everything to help accessorize your kilt, from sporrans (leather pouches) and sgians dubh (daggers) to special socks and shoes. Women's plaid skirts are also for sale. For a taste of Scotland, be sure to pick up a can or two of imported haggis.

The Scottish Tartan Museum (86 East Main Street; www.scottish tartans.org) is open from 10:00 A.M. to 5:00 P.M., Monday through Saturday. Franklin is located on Highway 441 in Macon County.

Rock On
Franklin

Ruby City Gems bills itself as "North Carolina's largest and finest gem and mineral shop." While a few other shops might take issue with that, very few could seriously challenge the claim.

An avid gem collector named Ernest Klatt opened the place in 1960, and over the years the goodies have stacked up. Containing both a store and a free museum, Ruby City displays hundreds of natural rarities. Some of the most notable items are choice Native-American relics, ivory carvings, intricate stone art pieces, authentic shrunken heads (yes, of humans), giant rubies, and what has been billed as "the world's largest sapphire"—a 385-pound hunk of glassy, glorious mineral.

The rock shop is located at 130 East Main Street in downtown Franklin and has seasonal hours. For details call (828) 524–3967 or visit www.rubycity.com.

THE MOUNTAINS

Livin' Large
Hendersonville

People of a certain age will remember a picture of two extremely big lads riding their minibikes away from the camera and into history through the pages of the *Guinness Book of World Records*.

Well, history has come to rest on the quiet hillside next to Crab Creek Baptist Church. The world's largest twins (a distinction often challenged but never surpassed) are sleeping peacefully beneath a granite marker as big as their reputation.

Benny and Billy McCrary didn't set out to be famous. For these modest country boys, being identical twins was plenty interesting. And then they began growing.

At age nine the boys were simultaneously laid low by an attack of the measles so severe that it damaged their pituitary glands. A year later each weighed more than 200 pounds. By the time they reached high school, they had topped 400 pounds and were a terror on their school's championship football team.

Finding work after graduation was hard, so they took to helping out their parents at home. From chore to chore they would ride a pair of minibikes. They soon began appearing on their minibikes in Hendersonville's Apple Festival and later in the year at Asheville's holiday parade. Local motorcycle shops started clamoring for them to advertise their wares, and from that point it was just a short leap to fame. The judges from Guinness found them and crowned them, and the McCrarys were off—appearing in Las Vegas, telling jokes, making music, and shilling with a 400-pound go-go dancer, a mere slip of a woman compared to Hendersonville's monumental duo. They became—what else?—professional wrestlers, with signature takedowns that often included minibikes as props.

They gained weight well into adulthood, breaking the 800-pound barrier before careful eating brought them down to a more sustainable 700 pounds. And lest one get the idea that an extraordinarily stout frame is simply money in the bank, the McCrarys' physiques posed no shortage of troubles for them. Beyond the hardship of finding clothes to fit (Benny's waist was 81 inches; Billy's, 84), they required cars with welded reinforcements to carry them on errands. They carried portable jacks with them from gig to gig to prop up their motel beds. They got so big that Billy once got trapped in an airplane restroom and had to be cut out following an emergency landing. "Living large" was less than glamorous, so they often talked of having operations to reduce their bulk.

But showbiz beckoned and they stayed with it. Then in 1979, during an appearance at Niagara Falls, Billy fell off his motorbike. He died of complications from the injury, and his body was returned to Hendersonville. Benny followed him in 2001. The boys' father, Frank B. J. "Throttle Boy" McCrary, rests nearby; their mother, Virginia G. McCrary, still lives near Hendersonville.

It takes a lot of granite to memorialize the big lives of the brothers McCrary.

Along with twin minibikes and sheaves of wheat, on Benny's side of their shared gravestone is an inscription describing him as "a kind hearted man spreading God's word in a big way." The inscription on Billy's side calls him "a legend as big as the mountains around him." A slab between them says "World Record Holders." Indeed.

Crab Creek Baptist Church is located at 72 Jeter Mountain Road. From Hendersonville, take US 64 West to Crab Creek Road; turn left onto Jeter Mountain Road.

Wolfe's Angel

Hendersonville

The late author Thomas Wolfe had, to indulge in a little pop psychology, "mother issues." It's not guessing to say that the overbearing guest-house keeper seemed to have been a major source of her son's melancholy and self-torture; rather, the proof is on every page.

So it's a little curious, perhaps, that the stone cherub that inspired the Asheville-born Wolfe's best-known book, *Look Homeward, Angel,* today sits atop the grave of a woman whose children seemed to have loved her wholeheartedly.

Wolfe's father operated a monument shop in Asheville, outside which the angel, carved by Italian sculptors, stood for years. Eventually the father sold it to mark the grave, in Oakdale Cemetery near Hendersonville, of Margaret E. Johnson, who lived from 1832 to 1935. Johnson was the wife of the Reverend H. H. Johnson, onetime president of Whitworth Female College in Brookhaven, Mississippi.

Husband and wife are buried beside each other in the gated plot. Beneath the angel's gentle reverie, an inscription on Johnson's grave reads that "her children arise up and call her blessed." The same couldn't be said of Wolfe, sorry to say.

William Faulkner considered Thomas Wolfe the most gifted writer of his age—high praise, considering the source. How nice that a vestige of the novelist's inspiration—however grave—is still on view.

Oakdale Cemetery is located about 2 miles west of downtown Hendersonville on US 64. The Johnson plot is sited on the left side of the road.

The angel that inspired Thomas Wolfe still hovers in Hendersonville.

The Mask Museum

Hendersonville

Retired art teacher Ellen Hobbs has traveled all around North and South America, Africa, and Asia, and each time has returned with masks. Today, she owns 500 of these creative face-covers in addition to dolls in various native garbs and a sampling of world textiles. The collection is ripe for the gazing at her Fifth Avenue Mask Museum in Hendersonville.

Despite her museum's uptown-sounding name, Hobbs is unpretentious and very eager to show off her collection. While Americans eschew masks most of the year (except during Halloween and while knocking off banks), in traditional cultures around the world masks are thought to cure ills, unite the wearer with ancestral spirits, or even transform them into wild animals. Hobbs's masks range from fearsome to comic and display a variety of dental arrangements—snaggle-toothed, tusked, and smiling benignly.

The Fifth Avenue Mask Museum is located at 317 Fifth Avenue West. To arrange a visit contact Hobbs at (828) 693–7108.

Among Ellen Hobbs's hundreds of masks, these seven from Indonesia tell the saga of good versus evil.

Ready to Rock

Hendersonville

Please don't hold us to it, but we're fairly confident that the Hendersonville Mineral & Lapidary Museum is the sole place in our great state where you can have a geode cracked while you wait.

"Geode," you ask? *Webster's New Universal Unabridged Dictionary* defines one as "hollow, concretionary or nodular stone often lined with crystals." The museum gets theirs from a particularly bleak, arid part of Chihuahua State in Mexico. For a sum varying according to size ($12 to $39), visitors can pick one out from a series of bins and have obliging museum volunteers crack it open with a stout device that involves a length of chain and formidable metal teeth.

Jurassic omelet: It's not every day you get to touch dinosaur eggs.

THE MOUNTAINS

On the day we visited, a handful of museum visitors gathered around for a cracking good time. A boy of about ten picked out a promising-looking geode from a bin and handed it to museum volunteer Robert Snowball, who placed it in the cracker and mashed down on a yard-long handle. With a flourish the plain rock was broken open, revealing an intricate, crystalline heart.

"Wow," the boy said, wide-eyed.

"It's 45 million years old, and you're the first person to see inside it," Snowball said, his British accent sounding tailor-made for the wonder of the moment.

Minutes later, Snowball said that occasionally fossil water dribbles out from the geodes' centers. "Reckon I should put it with a little whiskey and drink it, just to see what it tastes like," he said.

But you'd be wrong to believe that it's geodes-only at the rock museum. There is a display of luminescent rocks under glass tucked away behind a black curtain. If you press a button, a dignified female narrator describes "the wonders of fluorescence."

"Under normal daylight, the rocks in this display are downright ugly," she says. "Fluorescence transforms these ugly rocks into the spectacular beauties of the mineral world." And so it does.

There are other items to gaze upon: a mastodon tusk replica; fish fossils; a saber-toothed tiger skeleton; dinosaur fossils; plant fossils; bug fossils; ornate minerals; arrowheads of varying sizes from all over the country; petrified wood; figurines cut from jade, soapstone, onyx, cinnabar, and wood; jewelry; lots of coral; and a gift shop selling all manner of mini-minerals for the junior collector.

We were especially taken with a half dozen dinosaur eggs encased in Plexiglas with a hole allowing you to reach in and touch this peculiar bit of history. They look a little like something Fred Flintstone might pick up in a pinch at the convenience store.

The museum is located in the basement of 400 North Main Street. Hours are 1:00 to 5:00 P.M., Monday through Friday, and 10:00 A.M. to 5:00 P.M. Saturday. Call (828) 698–1977 or visit www.mineralmuseum .org for rock-solid directions.

Take a Little Trip
Hendersonville

It took dozens of years, millions of dollars, and the lives of scores of workers to build the railroads through western North Carolina's mighty mountains. Still, with fewer of us than ever riding the rails, today it's hard to get a sense of what a monumental feat of engineering and labor that construction really was.

Going miniature with Western North Carolina's topsy-turvy rail lines turns out to be a great way to put it all in perspective. Witness the main exhibit at the Historic Hendersonville Depot, home of the Apple Valley Model Railroad Club, and you'll get the idea. A 420-square-foot replica of the region's rail lines fills a main room of the facility, which is itself a 103-year-old, lovingly restored depot.

The replica's 800 feet of track travel through models of Hendersonville, Fletcher, Asheville, Canton, and Saluda. The highlight of the trip is the half-pint climb up the Saluda grade—the steepest main-line rail grade in the United States.

The depot is located at the corner of 7th Avenue and Maple Street in downtown Hendersonville. It's open on Saturday from 10:00 A.M. to 2:00 P.M. year-round, and on Wednesday from noon to 2:00 P.M. between Memorial Day and Labor Day. For more information e-mail info@avmrc.com or visit www.avmrc.com.

WHATEVER FLOATS YOUR BOAT

Col. Sidney Vance Pickens's dream of steamboating the French Broad River was dashed upon the rocks—well, upon the sand, to be precise.

In the years following the Civil War, Pickens, a Hendersonville resident and Confederate veteran, saw in the relatively shallow French Broad the potential for deep profits. With help from Congressman Robert Vance of Asheville, Pickens and other businessmen secured funding for the U.S. Army Corps of Engineers to dredge the river's shallowest spots between Brevard and Asheville. Then, Pickens proclaimed, he'd build a steamship to ferry passengers, products, and even the U.S. mail.

In 1881 Pickens completed his craft. The *Water Lily* was a simple but handsome ship. It was 90 feet long—big enough to accommodate two decks, two paddle wheels, and one hundred passengers—and painted white with green trim.

The maiden voyage, while quite short, was a smash, as a capacity crowd filled the boat and locals delighted at their first encounter with a steamboat whistle. Pickens boasted that his operation was "The Highest Steamboat Line in America," offering travelers a welcome alternative to navigating mountain roads on poky horse-drawn wagons.

But for all his hopes of forging an aquatic fortune, the river still proved ill-suited for the *Water Lily*. For one thing, although the river might have been deep enough for the boat, it was too narrow in spots for the *Water Lily* to pass through. And then there was King Bridge, which was too low for the boat to pass beneath.

So Pickens settled for making short runs for sightseeing, hosting parties, and the like. His French Broad Steamship Company slowly leaked money until 1885, when a flash flood tore the *Water Lily* from the riverbank and carried it away until it lodged on a sandbar.

It was the *Water Lily*'s last run, but not its final resting place. When the boat was dismantled, her wooden planks were used to construct the Riverside Baptist Church in Horse Shoe, where the good ship's bell was installed in the belfry.

The Goat Gland King

Laporte

This stone cottage in the Laporte community in Jackson County gives little hint of the reckless and wildly influential life of its former owner, Dr. John R. Brinkley.

Before men had drugs like Viagra and Cialis to put, as they say, "the lead back in their pencils," legitimate cures for erectile dysfunction were hard to come by. In that age of quackery, no one quacked quite as loud as Dr. Brinkley.

Born here in 1885 Brinkley grew up an underachieving student. Nevertheless, by 1918, with a string of medical degrees from unaccredited colleges under his belt, Brinkley set up a medical practice in Milford, Kansas. His specialty was "curing" impotence by stitching goat glands

The house that glands built.

into his patients, a procedure he was later estimated to have performed on 16,000 men. With capital amassed from his popular cure, in 1923 Brinkley built that state's first radio station, KFKB ("Kansas First, Kansas Best"). Ever the entrepreneur, he gave medical talks alongside the regular performances by local musicians, building his practice gland by valuable gland.

When officials caught wind of the good doctor's dubious earnings, they yanked his license to practice medicine. Brinkley answered by moving his practice to a hotel in south Texas. Across the border at Villa Acuña, Mexico, he built a powerful radio station—first XER, later XERA—whose signal could be heard as far away as Russia. The "border blaster" stations helped to popularize early country music stars like the Carter Family, as well as banjoist and singer Samantha Bumgarner, also a Jackson County native.

Some of Brinkley's programming choices were less inspired; in 1939 and 1940 he gave airtime to a string of Nazi sympathizers, including North Carolina–based William Dudley Pelley. The U.S. government soon had enough and in 1941 worked with the Mexican government to put Brinkley out of business.

Dogged by claims of tax evasion and drowning in malpractice suits, Brinkley died of a heart attack in May 1941 and was buried in Memphis, Tennessee.

The Laporte residence was built in 1929 when Brinkley was still a rising star. His surname is emblazoned in pale river rocks on the entrance gate. In 1937 Brinkley erected an elaborately carved stone monument to his beloved Aunt Sally, the woman who raised him. It stands about 1 mile north on Highway 107 on a shady bend of the road.

Brinkley's house is located on the northwest side of Highway 107, 1.1 miles north of State Road 1172. It is not open to the public.

Just-a-Swangin'

Linville

Grandfather Mountain's Mile High Swinging Bridge is perched 5,305 feet above sea level. The 228-foot, flexible bridge promises a thrill. It spans a very real 80-foot rock chasm and it *does* swing. At the caress of anything more than the merest zephyr, the bridge begins to tremble a little. Winds at Grandfather Mountain are notably fierce (they've been clocked at more than 200 mph), so during freak storms you might well reconsider crossing it. Furthermore, engineers refer to its design as "gravity anchored," a designation that hardly makes us sure-footed with confidence. A lot of people go white-knuckled at their first step and refuse to cross it, and you won't find us blaming these wimps.

This modest man-made wonder was built in 1952; it was fabricated at a Greensboro plant and then pieced together here at the mountaintop. It cost $15,000 at the time. In 1999 it was rebuilt with galvanized steel at a considerably inflated price—$300,000.

As you might imagine, the bridge is fully exposed to the weather, so in the colder months you'd be wise to dress warmly, here just a few hundred feet beneath Grandfather Mountain's very-exposed summit. A sign at the bridge's anchor warns that no more than forty people may cross at once. (You might want to find another spot for that staff photo, after all.)

Grandfather Mountain, a private attraction, is located on U.S. Highway 221, 2 miles north of Linville and 1 mile south of the Blue Ridge Parkway at milepost 305. For more information visit www .grandfather.com.

You Take the High Road

Linville

The Blue Ridge Parkway was begun in 1930, and all but 7.5 of its 469 miles were finished by 1967. The most obvious sticking point was a measly quarter-mile section skirting the landmark crag known as Grandfather Mountain.

The mountain's owner, Hugh Morton, was loath to see the National Park Service get a toehold on his beloved peak, and accordingly he made it very difficult for them to span it. For years the impasse required

No place for driver's ed: The Blue Ridge Parkway's Linn Cove Viaduct.

drivers to take a 14-mile detour along the Yonahlossee Trail (US 221). Tit for tat, the federal government answered by building a very difficult bridge here.

The Linn Cove Viaduct was begun in 1979 after years of delays and finished in 1983. It cost nearly $10 million and became widely known (around the world, in fact) as "the world's most complicated bridge."

Engineers blunted many a pencil designing the viaduct. The road runs past Grandfather Mountain at a dizzying height of 4,100 feet, and officials determined that, at such a high, fragile location, it was important to build the bridge without gouging a construction road into the venerable peak's flanks. The resulting 1,243-foot span was created out of 153 curved cement segments, each weighing 50 tons. The massive pieces were joined with epoxy glue, and then steel rods were threaded through to link them. Today, the parkway runs in a continuous curve along the bridge, which was tinted to match the surrounding rock. What'll they think of next?

The Linn Cove Viaduct is not only the world's most complicated bridge, but also, unsurprisingly, one of the parkway's most photographed spots. The National Park Service describes it as "safe but thrilling." Go ahead and find out for yourself, but please remember: hands on the steering wheel at 10 and 2.

The Linn Cove Viaduct Visitors Center, at milepost 304, offers restrooms, historical information, and access to a trail that takes you right under the bridge. Call the center at (828) 733–1354.

Hallelujah, They Saw the Lights
Linville Falls

In 1771 an obscure German sojourner named Gerard Will de Brahm passed along the flanks of Brown Mountain, the 2,600-foot ridge that divides Burke and Caldwell counties. De Brahm, like many before him, was startled and mesmerized by the strange lights he saw there. But unlike the others, he posited an explanation for them. They were, he wrote, caused by "nitrous vapors which are borne by the wind and, when laden winds meet each other, the niter inflames, sulphurates and deteriorates."

More than two centuries later, physicists, geologists, paranormal experts, and curious campers are no closer to a full explanation of why, exactly, the Brown Mountain Lights happen. Naturally, theories like de Brahm's, involving explosive, malodorous gases, still have traction—especially within the twelve-year-old-male demographic. Other possibilities have centered around magnetic variances, ball lightning, radium ore, and Saint Elmo's fire, the discharge of electrical current from conductive objects. But let's face it: No one knows what lies at their glowing heart.

Mysterious lights like Brown Mountain's make up one of the largest categories of unexplained phenomena, by some counts more popular than bleeding Christ figures, apparitions of the Virgin Mary, and storms of falling fish. The most famous lights in the United States are the Marfa Lights in dry, cattle-strewn west Texas.

The types of light peculiar to Brown Mountain have taken on a variety of forms, from small pinpoints to basketball-size circles that split apart, rejoin, and change color from red, to white, to blue (which, if not plausible, is at least patriotic).

Paranormal expert Josh Warren of the Asheville–based research team LEMUR insists that the lights grow from the electrical storage capacity of the layers of quartz and granite underlying the modest peak. The current makes its way to the surface as glowing plasma, says Warren, who has spent whole weeks studying the phenomenon from nearby viewpoints.

In contrast, Dan Caton, an Appalachian State University astronomy and physics professor, has studied the lights for a more than a dozen years, all to no avail. Caton today considers himself "the world's leading expert who's never seen them." He has turned his professorial eye on Brown Mountain during more than twenty separate viewing trips, accompanied by students and a colleague. And what has he seen? Nothing. Nada. Goose egg.

"The closest thing we saw was a brief, low-level flash of light down in the [Linville] gorge. We've been up there and heard people around us get excited about things that were clearly campfires and headlights. But people want to believe."

But don't let a guy like Dr. Caton spoil the fun. Go look for the lights yourself. There are three popular spots for light-gazing: the Brown Mountain Overlook, located 20 miles north of Morganton, on Highway 181, 1 mile south of the Barkhouse Picnic Area; Wiseman's View Overlook, located 5 miles south of the village of Linville Falls on Kistler Memorial Highway, aka Old Highway 105 or State Road 1238; and the Lost Cove Cliffs Overlook, located on the Blue Ridge Parkway at milepost 310, 2 miles north of the Highway 181 junction.

Eat My Fumes

Maggie Valley

The most impressive items at the Wheels Through Time museum are the unexpected ones. Sure, there are cool cars—a 1964 Cadillac once owned by *Stalag 13* star Steve McQueen, for instance, or the 1930 Caddy that folk-rocker Neil Young used to sport about in—but it's the other, more obscure gas-guzzlers that really turn heads.

Dale Walksler captains a one-bike motorcycle gang on "Big."

Consider, if you will, the ice cutter fashioned from a 1915 Harley-Davidson; the proto-personal watercraft propelled by a 1921 Harley-Davidson water-cooled engine; or the one-seater plane with a "hawg's" heart under its hood. Owner-curator Dale Walksler calls his "the museum that runs," and with horsepower like this at his disposal, we're not about to doubt him.

Walksler has held a passion for internal combustion thingies since childhood, and the thirty years' worth of collecting he's done while in the motorcycle business forms the core of the exhibit. He opened Wheels Through Time first in Mount Vernon, Illinois, where it thrilled visitors for two decades before Walksler decided to crate his holdings and head south. These days, about 50,000 people pass through the Maggie Valley attraction each year.

Wheels Through Time is located at 62 Vintage Lane in Maggie Valley. It's open daily from 9:00 A.M. to 6:00 P.M. Admission is $12.00 for adults, $10.00 for seniors, $6.00 for children ages five through twelve, and free for children four and under. For more information call (828) 926–6266 or visit www.wheelsthroughtime.com.

THE "DIRTY" DANCING GRANDMA

Western North Carolina is the proud home to the 1987 film *Dirty Dancing*, much of which was filmed in and around Lake Lure. But Marshall resident Rebecca Millis found out the hard way that at least one nearby town wasn't ready for people to really get down on the dance floor.

Millis was a regular at the town's Saturday night dances, which took place at a venue called the Marshall Depot. Some town residents complained to local authorities that the fifty-something grandmother was too provocative on the dance floor. She bent over too much, they said, and the skirts she wore were judged to be way too short.

In December 2000 Millis received a letter from the mayor of Marshall telling her that her moves were too suggestive and that she was from that point forward banned from the dance. If she showed up at another one, he warned, she'd be arrested.

Millis was one grandma who wasn't going to stand still. With help from North Carolina's chapter of the American Civil Liberties Union, she beat back the restriction in federal court.

"I'm an American citizen, I'm going to stand up for my rights," she said. "So what if I have a different style of dancing from everyone else? I just hear the music and start moving."

Word Up
Murphy

You could drive the world round and never see a sight as awe-inspiring as the giant Ten Commandments at Fields of the Wood.

God's best-known set of rules covers a whole hillside here, with individual letters in poured cement as tall—taller, even—than your Uncle Ed.

We arrived on a warmish summer day and were exhausted and breathless by the time we'd climbed up the hill as far as the First Commandment, THOU SHALT HAVE NO OTHER GODS BEFORE ME. We failed to count the steps on the way up, but suffice it to say they were many.

Fields of the Wood Bible Park, as the place is properly known, is the spiritual home to the Pentecostal denomination known as the Church of God of Prophecy. It was on this site, in 1903, that a group of twenty-one believers gathered at the home of W. F. Bryant and pledged to accept the Bible as the perfect, inerrant word of God. That accomplished, they gave themselves a name, the Church of God of the Bible. Twenty years later the church split, and the faction that became the Church of God of Prophecy built the park here in 1941. The church's headquarters today are in Jonesborough, Tennessee.

The Ten Commandments (reputed to be the largest representation in any of the four hemispheres) may be the most impressive display at the park, but there are other must-sees. There is Prayer Mountain, another calf-burner of a climb. The path up is marked with stones donated by churches from the various states, all with weighty scriptures printed on them. As you climb, the views behind you are to the Ten Commandments—a handy thing if you should feel yourself backsliding.

Among the park's other attractions are a baptismal pool that looks inviting and a life-size mock-up of Golgotha, the hill where Jesus and the thieves were crucified, which looks somewhat less so. Nearby, a series of boxwood shrubs are trimmed to read JESUS DIED FOR OUR SINS.

There is a tomb with a massive wooden "stone" that can be rolled back and forth. Inside the tomb is a greasy figure beneath a cotton shroud, mounted to a stretcher. Jesus, we presume?

The gift shop is well appointed with Fields of the Wood merchandise, and less specific Christian goods and literature. A snack shop shares the space, a welcome sight should all the inspiration work up a hunger in you. Thousands visit the park each year; admission is free.

To get to Fields of the Wood, take US 64 west through Murphy to Highway 294. The park is located 9.8 miles up Highway 294, on the right.

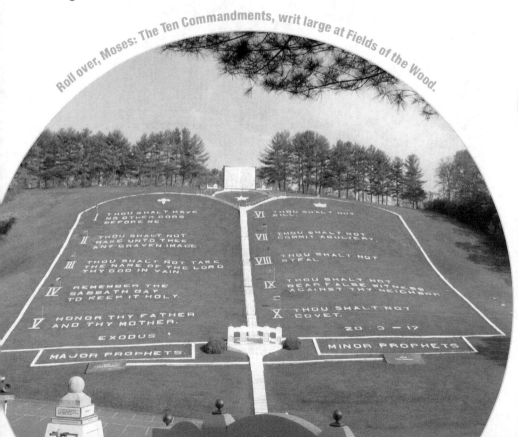

Roll over, Moses: The Ten Commandments, writ large at Fields of the Wood.

The End of Rudolph's Run

Murphy

Most folks expected Eric Rudolph, America's most wanted serial bomber, to go out with a bang. Instead, the elusive target of a five-year, $30 million manhunt got caught Dumpster-diving by a rookie cop.

It was the wee hours of Sunday, May 31, 2003. Rudolph—who now admits that he bombed abortion clinics, a gay nightclub, and a site at the 1996 Olympics in Atlanta—had found that being a federal fugitive meant living off the food he could forage from spots near his secluded mountain campsites.

A meal fit for a bomber: The Dumpster where the law caught up with Eric Rudolph.

THE MOUNTAINS

A year after his capture, Rudolph detailed the events of that night in a letter to his mother, which *USA Today* quoted shortly thereafter. "It was a Saturday night . . . a good night for garbage," he wrote.

Rudolph explained how he painstakingly made his way from his camp to the back of the town of Murphy's Sav-A-Lot grocery, where he'd found a regular supply of free vittles in the trash bin. He had survived a close call on a previous food-gathering mission, he told his mother. "One night, while I was hiding in the Dumpster at Taco Bell, [a police officer] got out of his car, went into the Dumpster area and (urinated) on the Dumpster I was hiding in."

For all his vigilance Rudolph caught some bad luck on his final night of freedom. Officer Jeffrey Postell pulled up behind the Sav-A-Lot just as the fugitive approached the Dumpster. The bomber described the scene to his mother: "I think about running, about the headache of hiding, the many nights rooting through garbage, the 10 degrees below zero days when I sit in my tent all day and shiver; and I decide that I don't care. It was meant to happen." Rudolph was arrested without a fight.

Three years after Rudolph got snared, we visited the Sav-A-Lot that ended his life on the lam. In the parking lot we asked a young man gathering shopping carts if we were at the right place.

"Yep, the Dumpster's in back," he said. "Some nights, it was locked—and you can still see the marks where he tried to break into it."

What would the rogue bomber find there today, we wondered, if he was still on the run? So we climbed about Rudolph's favorite Dumpster and inventoried its bountiful contents: a crate of Nature's Delight cabbage, six bunches of bananas (reduced for quick sale), some yellowed broccoli, a box of Quick Links Beef and Cheddar Sausage, and a real find for dessert—an unopened, one-pound bag of Wild Berry Skittles. Now that's good fugitive eatin'.

Would-be visitors to the site, take note: The Sav-A-Lot recently changed its name to Super Saver. The store is located at 128 West Main Street in Murphy; the Dumpster is behind it.

A Hairy Situation
Old Fort

"Bigfoot." "Sasquatch." Whatever you call him, he's a beast of burden for a small but intense bunch of searchers, one of whom swore he saw the Big Hairy One—and several times, at that—near Old Fort.

In 1999 Tom Burnette self-published *Nature's Secret Agents,* a 120-page tale of wonder and woe. In it he described his yearslong quest to bait, connect with, and capture images of the Bigfoot(s) he was sure shared his mountainside, and his frustrated efforts to convince the world of his crypto-zoological find.

"Friend or Foe?" he asked on the first page. In the end Burnette chose "friend." But getting there with Bigfoot wasn't exactly easy. "The only reason this book was written is because the events which surrounded me were too unbelievable and almost unrealistic for myself or anyone else for that matter to comprehend or understand," he wrote.

That's a fair summation. Burnette's book is an incredible chronicle of anecdotes and photos that might leave most Bigfoot-fetishers wondering just what, exactly, he really saw and interacted with.

But still, he went to a lot of trouble along the way—scrutinizing hundreds of blurry photographs, strands of hair, and animal droppings. So if you find yourself wandering in the woods near Old Fort, keep a sharp eye out for size-19 footprints and hairy, hulking figures in the mist. "You cannot discover the whole world from a textbook," Burnette fittingly wrote in the book's "Final Thought." "Sometimes you have to reach out and become part of nature herself in order to learn and discover."

Andrews Geyser
Old Fort

Sometimes a man just wants to spurt a sizable shaft of water into the air.

And so it was for the executives at Southern Railway, the company that built the railroad through perilous mountain patches of western North Carolina. For decades the rail line had stopped dead in Old Fort, as engineers had not yet conjured the means to take trains through the peaks and valleys just to the west.

But in the 1870s Southern Railway put the pedal to the metal, as a colorful company vice president, Col. A. B. Andrews, spearheaded the effort to build rails up the mountains. He pulled it off—but it took more than three years to get through one serpentine 3-mile stretch. Meanwhile, the work proved so dangerous that more than 200 men lost their lives in the undertaking.

That stretch completed, the Southern Railway honchos decided to do something to commemorate all those who had died. After some discussion they settled on a man-made geyser—it seemed a natural choice, given that the area was replete with creeks, rivers, and quick drops in altitude.

A prime location was selected: a spot sitting in a small valley that is all but surrounded by the railroad, which meanders through the hills above almost a full 360 degrees around the geyser. If you're there when one of the longer trains rolls through, you get the pleasant feeling that you're a miniature figurine in the middle of a model train set.

And, oh yeah—you'll also get to take in a mighty, misty column of mountain water that shoots straight up to around 70 feet, twisting a bit in the wind, while at the same time always raining down. Andrews Geyser, named for the man who drove the railroad through, is free, open to the public, and surrounded by a sizable concrete wading pool that's a super spot to get your mist on.

Isaac Newton would be proud: Gravity is the sole force powering this fun fountain. All it takes is a strategically placed dam on a mountain creek and some good pipe to carry the water down a steep mountain face.

To get there from nearby Old Fort, take US 70 West (for 0.3 mile) to Old US 70. Turn right and travel 2.4 miles to Mill Creek, where you turn right and go 2.1 miles. Andrews Geyser will be the aquatic eruption to your left.

Mist opportunity: At Andrews Geyser, you can get wet every day.

A Mountain Welcome

Old Fort

Most folks who make their way to North Carolina's mountains pass through Old Fort, a railroad/mill town at the base of Interstate 40's climb toward Black Mountain and Asheville. And most of them speed on through, stopping briefly for gas or grub, if they stop at all. If they would venture just a mile into town, they could get a free taste of just what is so weird and wonderful about mountain dwellers.

Downtown Old Fort's Mountain Gateway Museum is a modest delight operated as part of the official state museum system. Set on an acre of riverside land, the facility has a museum proper, an outdoor amphitheater, and several historic outbuildings—log cabins and such—that offer a quick journey back in time.

In the museum itself the curators aren't shy about showing the full spectrum of mountain life, from the mundane to the extraordinary. More-or-less permanent exhibits include a display of what today would be called "primitive" mountain medicines (even though some have since made their way into widespread use) and a life-size replica of a moonshine still. Be warned: The latter display features an unusually life-like stuffed rattlesnake that'll sneak up on you—leaving us to wonder if the rattler serves as a not-so-subtle reminder that making moonshine remains a legal no-no.

The museum also features a series of temporary exhibits. During one visit we gaped at a small but remarkable collection of mountain funeral relics. Dubbed "Settin' Up with the Dead," the collection included poignant pendants made from the hair of deceased loved ones and explained the tradition of spending a little quality time with the recently departed.

For all its small wonders, Mountain Gateway seems to be something of a little-utilized gem. On the sunny spring day we first went there, the place was empty of visitors and staffed by only one person, who happened to be asleep at her desk. We called to her gently, and she awoke in good fashion. "Whew," she said, shaking off the nap. "It's been a really slow Saturday."

To reach Mountain Gateway, take I–40 to exit 73 into downtown Old Fort and follow the signs to the museum, at 102 Water Street. Hours are noon to 5:00 P.M. on Monday, 9:00 A.M. to 5:00 P.M. Tuesday through Saturday, and 2:00 to 5:00 P.M. on Sunday. For more information call (828) 668–9259 or visit www.ncmuseumofhistory.org/osm/mgw.html.

You're "still" the same: Makin' booze at the Mountain Gateway Museum.

Good for What Ails Ye
Robbinsville

The Cherokee, who once lived throughout western North Carolina as well as the upcountry of South Carolina and Georgia, had a deep connection to the natural world. Their way of life, right down to their system of medicine, depended heavily on what the woods provided.

And so they had touch-me-not to sooth the blisters of poison ivy, persimmon to treat diarrhea, wild ginger to settle a colicky baby, bone-set to mend broken bones, and rattlesnake plantain to relieve the pain of a toothache, to name only a smattering.

Many of these native cures—seventy-five, actually—are on display along the Cherokee Medicine Trail, which opened in 2002 just off Main Street in Robbinsville. Trails wind up through the shady woods, where tags mark plants vital to Cherokee medicine and describe their uses.

Ethnographer James Mooney lived among the Cherokee during the latter part of the nineteenth century and, in his book *The Sacred Formulas of the Cherokees,* outlined the tribe's healing arts. According to Mooney, Cherokee shamans (healers, wise men) had between 300 and 400 plants at their disposal when treating sickness and administering tonics.

"Western" medicine may look askance at many of the Cherokee's cures, but even today many of the most promising drugs continue to be found in plants. It's only natural, right?

The Cherokee Medicine Trail is located at 1 Junaluska Drive in Robbinsville. Call (828) 479–4727 or visit www.cherokeeheritagetrails.org for information.

Land of the Sky Spies
Rosman

In the remote reaches of many mountain communities, the rest of the world can seem very far away. Not so in Rosman, a small town just down the road from Brevard that hosts an extraordinary astronomical facility buried amid rhododendrons, jagged rocks, and bubbling streams. Here, the whole universe comes into reach.

The Pisgah Astronomical Research Institute (PARI) was founded in 1999. Fast becoming one of the most advanced independent science facilities in the country, the thirty-building complex is spread across a 200-acre, bowl-shaped clearing in the Pisgah National Forest.

PARI occupies unique ground, in more ways than one. In June 1963 NASA opened a base at the location to assist with expanded space flights, which President Kennedy was pushing for. The Rosman Satellite Tracking Station conducted its first mission in November 1963—the month Kennedy died—following the orbit of an unmanned craft sent up to check radiation levels in space. The station then collected data from the first generation of weather and atmospheric satellites and assisted the historic Gemini and Apollo missions.

With the rise of satellite technology, however, the Rosman station gradually became less useful, and in 1981 NASA pulled out.

Shortly thereafter, the National Security Agency (NSA) quietly took over the facility. The NSA conducts the government's most advanced espionage, making and breaking codes and intercepting mostly foreign (but sometimes domestic) communications. In recent years it has become controversial both at home and abroad due to concerns about privacy in personal communications.

Back then, the agency's main target was the Soviet Union's satellite communications, a most sensitive subject. When an *Asheville Citizen-Times* photographer stopped near the Rosman station's gate and

Dishing it out: At PARI, students shoot for the stars.

snapped a few pictures in 1985, FBI agents paid a visit to the newspaper's office to have a word.

In 1995, with the Cold War fading into history, the NSA left Rosman. The U.S. Forest Service took control of the land and made plans to raze the structures. But then Don Cline of Greensboro, an astronomy buff, stepped in to buy the place and establish PARI, which is now a nonprofit research institute.

With a full-time staff of 16 and some 200 volunteers, PARI today is a hotbed of astronomical research of many stripes, working with universities from throughout the state and the nation to study and understand the universe. Still, vestiges of PARI's cloistered, classified past are everywhere: underground tunnels, panes of bulletproof glass, and even a leftover trash can in the employee cafeteria, which is spray-painted with the words UNCLASSIFIED WASTE ONLY.

For more information about PARI, which is open to the public only on visitors' days, visit www.pari.edu.

Something to Bark About

Saluda

You may be nothing but a hound dog—but if so, scamper off to Saluda, where you'll be the center of attention every summer at Coon Dog Day.

For the past forty-three years, Saluda has hosted a daylong free-for-all of food, floats, and a lively, loud collection of canines. It's an occasion where every dog gets his day (every coon dog, that is), and the people have plenty of fun, too. The 2006 Coon Dog Day drew an estimated 15,000 visitors to watch the parade, run in the Coon Dog Day 5K, munch on fair fare, dance to live music, and, most of all, let the dogs do their thing.

From the perspective of the curiosity-seeker—and of many devoted locals, for that matter—the main event is surely the barking contest, which is held mid-afternoon. It's an elaborate but thoroughly enjoyable homegrown ritual.

Here's how it works: Coon dog owners bring their best and brightest pets to the field next to Saluda Elementary. At the appointed moment someone hoists a caged, stuffed raccoon up and down a pulley affixed atop a 15-foot pole. Each dog has exactly one minute to go after the mock prey, and the contestant's barks are counted by a four-man team of referees. The dog that utters the most barks at the raccoon, demonstrating why he's the one to hunt with, wins. At the most recent contest, the winning number was fifty-three.

Along the way there's some good-natured betting on which dog will sound off the most, and lots and lots of barking.

Coon Dog Day is held every July in Saluda. For a full schedule visit www.saluda.com or call (828) 749–2581.

The Writing's on the Rock
Sylva

Cherokee lore speaks of a "slant-eyed giant" named Judaculla who, when he wasn't busy striding across the mountains step by gargantuan step, liked to doodle on rocks. Of course this was years ago, before giants' lives became so very busy. What remains of Judaculla's handiwork sits today next to Jerry Parker's driveway in a cattle-grazed creek bottom, a half mile off a state road.

Judaculla Rock is big, brown, and mysterious. The soapstone boulder measures roughly 16 feet by 11 feet. Its surface is etched with swirls and straight lines and more specific designs that seem to represent turtles and salamanders. The oddest ones look like octopuses (or seven-fingered hands, depending on where you're standing).

See it before it's gone: Prehistoric Judaculla Rock is slip slidin' away.

There is a "see-it-now" urgency about the rock, though; its surface is eroding fast, and no one, it seems, is overly concerned with preserving it. Some years ago, Jackson County built a viewing platform and a series of displays near the rock to give the place a little more formality, but other than a few yellowed newspaper clippings and some carvings along the railing of more recent vintage (JEANNE, DUSTIN, MELISSA G., etc.), there's not much to see.

But the rock itself is well worth the trip. The western states are brimming with this sort of ancient rock carvings, which are called petroglyphs, but they are much less common in the humid East. Judaculla Rock is North Carolina's only easily viewed sizable petroglyph, and it ranks as a nationally important archaeological site.

Archaeologists have dated the carvings to the Archaic Period (3000–1000 B.C.), but haven't yet determined their exact origin or meaning.

So, for now, we'll stick with the Judaculla explanation. The Cherokee considered him a "Great Lord of the Hunt," but the evidence in front of us suggests he also had artistic leanings and was a Renaissance man well before his time. There is a thick screen of river cane behind the rock, and it's easy to believe, if you let yourself, that the slant-eyed giant will return from within it at any minute, snack on a cow, and put a few finishing touches on his masterpiece. Who knows? Maybe he'll tidy the place up a bit while he's at it.

To get to Judaculla Rock, take US 74 to Business Route 23 through Sylva. Stay on Route 23 for 1.3 miles and then turn left onto Highway 107. Drive 8 miles on Highway 107 and take a left onto Caney Fork Road. Go 2.5 miles and turn left onto a gravel road. The rock is on the right about a half mile ahead. No carving, spray-painting, or even sitting on the rock, please. It's having a hard enough time already.

Say a Little Prayer

Trust

It takes a long, slow trek up winding mountain roads to reach St. Jude's Chapel of Hope, but if you believe in miracles, this pilgrimage is well worth it.

St. Jude's, you see, was built to mark a miracle: Beverly Barutio's unexpected recovery from the advanced stages of cancer. Diagnosed in 1981, the then–Florida resident underwent eleven rounds of chemotherapy over the course of the next year. Still, the cancer seemed unstoppable, and the discomfort caused by the treatments caused Barutio to stop them.

When all hope seemed lost, she turned to God, as she would later explain—and subsequent checkups revealed no sign of the disease. "The praying worked," she said. "I am a miracle."

So Barutio decided it was her duty to pay something back. "I promised St. Jude—he's the saint of hopeless and impossible causes—him and God and my husband, that one day I'd build a chapel. Over the years, I'd feel more and more strongly about it." After moving to the tiny mountain town of Trust in North Carolina, the Barutios in 1991 completed St. Jude's Chapel of Hope, which to this day remains open to the public at all hours of every day.

The 12-by-14-foot structure is a small wonder of sizable charm. Made of cedar, the chapel features stained-glass windows, four small, polished pews, a prayer bench and shrine to St. Jude, and even a bell in the belfry. A Bible sits open on the bench, and in front of it the shrine glistens with candles and small objects—trinkets, buttons, pictures, shells, and stones—left by visitors.

It's a quiet, meditative place, with sunlight streaming warm colors through the windows. A nondenominational church, St. Jude's lets visitors decide how to practice their spirituality, which is how Beverly

Small prayers go a long way at St. Jude's Chapel of Hope.

wanted it. She passed away in 2002, but the chapel remains in fine shape and continues to fulfill her mission. "If just one person comes over the mountain and it gives them a moment's peace, it has done what it was intended to do," she said when it was completed. "It's about giving something back to the world for what you've been given."

Beverly and her husband, Bill, didn't stop there. Today, visitors can also take in two other unique mountain attractions situated near the chapel. Down the hill a large wooden cross is set into a rustic stone base. A sign on it reads, FEAR NOT TOMORROW, JESUS IS ALREADY THERE. And across a gushing creek sits the lovely "Bridge of Madison County," a quaint covered bridge that pays a small homage to the novel and movie *The Bridges of Madison County*.

The Chapel of Hope sits near the intersection of Route 209 and Highway 63, about 30 miles northwest of Asheville.

A Morris, of Course
Tryon

Every town, no matter how small, needs a mascot. Tryon (population 1,760), is proud to have Morris, an outsize toy horse with a history full of more plot twists than a spy novel.

In the first part of the twentieth century, this little town in Polk County, not far from the South Carolina border, was home to a business called Tryon Toymakers and Woodcarvers. In 1928 the company fashioned a jumbo version of one of its most popular toys, a colorful horse with casters so that it could be rolled about, for the Tryon Riding & Hunt Club. The club began using the giant toy horse to advertise upcoming events.

Disaster struck (as it so often does) during the 1930s, when the building that housed the horse burned. A new horse took its place but was in turn stolen in 1946 by a couple of joy-riding wags whose jar (or two) of moonshine had them feeling their oats.

Age and exposure claimed its replacement in the 1960s. In 1983 the next replacement had nearly succumbed to age and exposure when locals gave it a total makeover, including a drum-shaped torso fashioned from marine-grade fiberglass.

So far, so good. This most recent incarnation of Morris, as locals long ago took to calling him, looks pretty darn good in this, his fourth decade. Now and again, we're told, the *Tryon Daily Bulletin* prints a letter from a reader who has spent a little time talking to Morris. (No mention of moonshine.) The horse's name, if you're a doubter, is stamped on a small metal tag beneath his neck.

Tryon is a one-horse town.

KINGDOM OF THE HAPPY LAND

What would compel a group of people to christen their community with the giddy name "The Kingdom of the Happy Land"? Freedom from lifelong bondage, that's what.

It may sound like something out of a children's book, but instead it was a name chosen by grateful grownups—former slaves from Mississippi, Alabama, Georgia, South Carolina, North Carolina, and other states who set up a Reconstruction-era outpost in Henderson County. Their experiment with forging a self-sustaining community survived barely a generation, but extraordinary tales of the Kingdom, fragmentary as they are today, continue to inspire.

The story begins in the days directly after the Civil War ended in 1865, when groups of freedmen and freedwomen left their masters behind and migrated toward a new life. The odds were stacked against them—while technically free, the former slaves still had plenty of white supremacy to overcome. But in some places they managed to carve out the space to set up safe, productive lives.

The Kingdom, which was located on and next to mountainsides in Tuxedo, not far from Hendersonville, was one of those places. Much of what is known about the community today is found in a seventeen-page monograph published by Asheville-based historian Sadie Smathers Patton in 1959. In it she recounted all that she was able to learn about the Kingdom by talking to the descendants of those who had staked a claim there.

Calling the story "a dim, tattered page of the history of Henderson County," Patton admitted that the limited number of records and firsthand recollections of the Kingdom made her study necessarily incomplete. But she was able to reconstruct the basics of how this unique realm came to be and what occurred there.

The Kingdom, which existed from roughly 1865 to 1900, was "governed by rulers known as King and Queen," Patton wrote, at the same time noting that affairs were generally run in a communal fashion in which "each man and woman filled every daylight hour with the common task of developing a new world for all."

The residents of the Kingdom, Patton found, migrated to the spot in a wagon train that swelled in numbers as it wended its way to North Carolina. Eventually they numbered in the many hundreds. Together they built log cabins, grew their own food on a collectivist farm, and sold extra vegetables to neighbors. They studied and worshipped together and formed choirs that performed for neighbors both white and black. They even marketed their own medicine: Happy Land Liniment, which Patton described as "a remedy for rheumatism, aching muscles and bones."

Though today the remnants are few, the Hendersonville–based Environmental and Conservation Organization (ECO) leads the occasional authorized tour of the land that was the Kingdom, which is on private property. Call ECO at (828) 692–0385 or visit www.eco-wnc .org to find out about opportunities to walk part of the wooded hills that were once home to this remarkable settlement.

Each Christmas, the giant toy horse gets a draping of holiday gar-
lands and a top hat, in the spirit of the season. Beyond decoration and
a reference point ("Just down the road, turn right at the horse"), Morris
also is used, as he has been from the outset, to advertise events for the
Riding & Hunt Club. He stands in the heart of the downtown, right
alongside a railroad grade crossing.

A Cross to Bear

Waynesville

The Christian cross appears in all shapes and sizes, from the tiniest
necklace pendant to hulking reproductions in and above churches. In
North Carolina few renditions loom as large as the Mount Lyn Lowry
Cross, which is perched on a 6,280-foot-high mountaintop that strad-
dles the line between Haywood and Jackson Counties, not far from
Waynesville.

Tampa native Lyn Lowry was a mere fifteen years old when she died
of leukemia in 1962. Her parents, retired Army Lieutenant General
Sumpter Lowry and Ivilyn Lowry, were wracked with sorrow but determined to create a legacy for Lyn. They picked one of her favorite vaca-
tion spots, a mountain peak in western North Carolina, to build a
permanent memorial to their departed daughter.

On the night of August 6, 1964, they flipped a switch and turned on
the lights that have lit up the cross on "Mount Lyn Lowry" ever since.
It's 60 feet tall, is illuminated at night, and can be seen from as far away
as 30 miles, if you're looking from the right direction.

One year later, the famed western North Carolina–based evangelist
Billy Graham traveled to the cross to offer a dedication. "I am sure we
all have mixed emotions as we stand on this glorious mountaintop," he
said. "We have tears in our eyes as we miss the loved one who was

taken from us. On the other hand, we rejoice that out of her death has come this symbol of the pure and wonderful life she led."

Most folks see the cross, which is maintained by a family foundation, from one of two vantage points. First of all, you can hike there. "The climb is but a small price to pay to be among the sky, the trees, the surrounding peaks and valleys below, the great cross above," notes a pamphlet published by the Haywood County Chamber of Commerce shortly after the cross went up. "It's glorious."

Another, less strenuous way to take in the soft-glowing cross is to drive at night along U.S. Highway 19/74 between Waynesville and Balsam Gap. On a clear night it's hard to miss. There's also an overlook on the Blue Ridge Parkway, at milepost 445.2, that offers a clear, if remote, view.

Ramping It Up

Waynesville

These are heady days for the ramp, that formerly humble Appalachian spring tonic turned haute cuisine ingredient. Ramps are a wild relative of the leek and are native to coves and moist woods from Quebec to Georgia. Historically, they've served as a welcome dose of spring greenery in diets propped up by salt pork. Today, none other than Martha Stewart says she loves gathering the plants, and TV chef Emeril Lagasse, too, has turned into a booster-come-lately for the pungent herb.

That's all well and good, but you can bet that all the celebrity attention hasn't gone to the heads of the organizers of the Haywood County Ramp Convention, whose predecessors were stuffing tow sacks with the wild onions decades before Martha Stewart was a twinkle in her daddy's eye. The celebration, which returns each May, remains mulishly old-fashioned as it approaches its seventy-fourth year.

The convention is sponsored by the Haywood Post #47 of the

American Legion. Ramps are sold both raw and cooked, in a variety of dishes, including the traditional scrambled eggs with ramps and potatoes with ramps. Bluegrass and the sounds of clogging also fill the air, mingling with the curiously pungent smell of ramps. Proceeds from the gathering go to local charities.

The event's highlight is the crowning of ramp royalty, the king and queen. The man who would be king must emerge victorious from the ramp-eating contest, in which whoever eats the most two-ounce bags of ramps wins. "When they say 'Go,' it's something you never want to see again," says Legion Commander Frank Lauer.

The Ramp Queen earns her tiara and sash by more genteel means. A week before the convention, the contestants submit essays outlining their aspirations and suitability for the role. "They'd probably have to love a ramp," notes Clint Smith, the convention's organizer.

The taste of ramps is reckoned to lie somewhere between onion and garlic, but the persistent bouquet of the raw ramp on the consumer's body is unique in most people's experience. "My husband used to take these spring trout-fishing trips all through the mountains with his friends," says Jeanine Davis, specialty crops coordinator with North Carolina State University. "They would eat ramps for basically every meal. He'd come home and I'd make him sleep on the couch for a few days."

"Once a year's about enough for ramps for me," says Smith. "Trust me—once you spend about a month out there gathering and cleaning the things and you're about psycho."

Good fun never smelled so bad. To catch a whiff of next year's convention, visit www.waynesvillelive.com.

Christmas in July
West Jefferson

Ho, ho, ho—happy Independence Day!

Wait a minute. What's Santa doing in a North Carolina mountain town in the middle of the year?

Well, he's celebrating his favorite holiday, only six months early. The good people of West Jefferson, many of whom make their present-buying money from selling Christmas trees, have good reason to celebrate the holiday twice a year. They call the summer version "Christmas in July."

Held every year on the weekend closest to July 4, the event has a little something for everyone, from Christmas crafts and ornaments to old-time music to an appearance by St. Nick himself. (He's probably glad to pay a visit when things aren't so frigid—and to get away from the toy-making grind for a couple of days.)

For the details on next year's festival, call the Ashe County Chamber of Commerce at (336) 846–9196 or visit www.christmasinjuly.info.

Worshipping al Fresco

West Jefferson

Sometimes the most beautiful things in the world arrive as an answer to prayer. No, we're not talking about the makings of some teenage romance movie here. We're talking about the Ashe County frescoes: wall paintings in the Classical Realist style that line the walls of two churches right off the foot of the Blue Ridge.

Back in the 1970s, after seeing attendance at St. Mary's Episcopal Church, in West Jefferson, and Holy Trinity Episcopal Church, in Glendale Springs, slide to a dismal low, Father Faulton Hodge had a few hard decisions to make. One was, of course, how to boost membership. The other was how to salvage Holy Trinity Church, where the sanctuary itself was caving in.

Strangers took care of both dilemmas. One day a man drove up to Hodge on a visit to his mother's home church and asked the priest how much repairs to Holy Trinity would cost. Hodge said $1,500. The man wrote him a check for that amount and drove off.

Later, at a dinner party, Hodge had a fortuitous meeting with Ben Long, a young artist in need of some large—very large—canvases to paint on. Long was ready to paint some frescoes—wall paintings made with ground pigment and lime (like the Sistine Chapel). What's more, he was willing to do it for free.

The Statesville-born Long wasn't some art school upstart. After studies at the University of North Carolina–Chapel Hill and the Art Student's League in New York, he had traveled to Italy, where he apprenticed for seven years to master artist Pietro Annigoni and developed a command of the techniques of both fresco painting and restoration.

Long painted his first frescoes in the diminutive St. Mary's Church. For *Mary, Great with Child,* he used his wife, who was pregnant at the time, as the model for the Holy Mother's body. For Mary's face he used the likeness of a girl he passed on a local street. Other frescoes depict the mystery of the resurrection.

At Holy Trinity Church, Long used both students and local townspeople as models for his depiction of the Last Supper.

The frescoes have gone on to become a significant attraction, bringing thousands of visitors to the two churches each year.

The paintings are visible year-round, and no admission is charged; however, donations are greatly appreciated. Across the street a gift shop sells an array of very inspired knickknacks—all to support the churches and their frescoes.

A Festival of the Frescoes is held at Holy Trinity Church each October. For more information, or to make group reservations, call (336) 982–3076. The churches' Web site address is www.churchofthe rescoes.com.

St. Mary's Episcopal Church is located on the north side of US 221, 0.1 mile west of State Road 1147 at Beaver Creek. Holy Trinity is located on the east side of State Road 1161, opposite State Road 1160, in Glendale Springs.

THE PIEDMONT

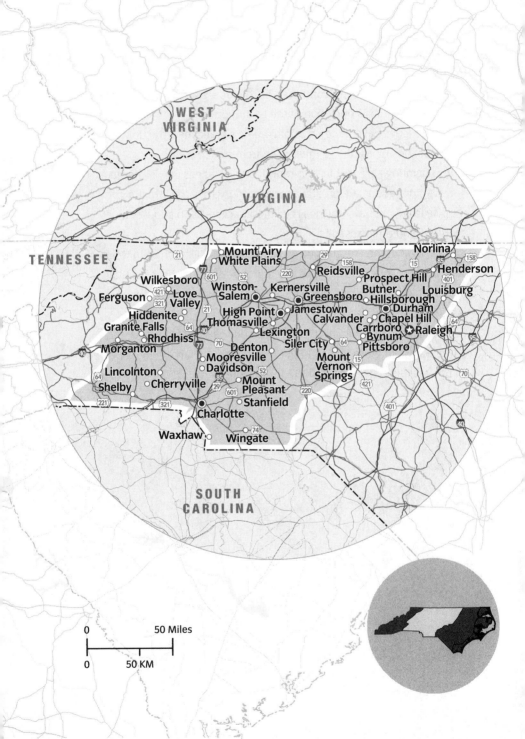

WEST
VIRGINIA

VIRGINIA

TENNESSEE

Mount Airy
White Plains
Reidsville
Norlina
Henderson
Prospect Hill
Butner
Louisburg
Wilkesboro
Winston-
Salem
Kernersville
Greensboro
Hillsborough
Ferguson
Love
Valley
Durham
Hiddenite
High Point
Jamestown
Chapel Hill
Granite Falls
Thomasville
Calvander
Carrboro
Raleigh
Rhodhiss
Lexington
Bynum
Morganton
Siler City
Pittsboro
Denton
Mount
Vernon
Springs
Mooresville
Davidson
Lincolnton
Cherryville
Mount
Pleasant
Shelby
Stanfield
Charlotte
Waxhaw
Wingate

SOUTH
CAROLINA

0   50 Miles

0   50 KM

THE PIEDMONT

We defy anyone to offer a tidy definition of the many and varied Tar Heels who make their homes in the Piedmont, North Carolina's most populated region. Suffice it to say that if you know where to look, you can find just about anything here.

Sometimes, we knew; other times, we just got lucky. Now *you* know, so there's no excuse for not hitting the road and letting us take you along for the ride.

It pays to be prepared for the Piedmont's quirks and curios. For example, you should steel yourself for the cigarette-boosting Tobacco History Museum in Durham, a city where you can also take in a terrific number of tubas, lemurs, and ESP practitioners.

But you're just getting started. Consider just a few of the Piedmont's extraordinary spectacles: There's Ricky Pearce's ginormous set of legs in Henderson, Alan Huffman's stupendous soda machine collection in Granite Falls, the late Henry Warren's mini Shangri-La in Prospect Hill, the Devil's Tramping Ground in Chatham County, and the Carnivore Preservation Trust's big game preserve in Pittsboro.

Heck, we almost forgot to mention what may be the Piedmont's most momentous contribution to curiosity culture: monuments to furniture. Yes, furniture. We kid you not: If you want to see the world's largest chair and chest of drawers, or talk to a tree in a furniture museum, then Piedmont's your place. And rest assured that here, at least, no one's going to hold your curiosity against you.

Critter Crossing

Bynum

There are folk artists, and then there are folk artists. Which is to say that some artsy types toil in obscurity, obsessively creating works that few members of the public will see—and then there are the kind that let their art roam free.

Clyde Jones is decidedly the latter type. If you take a drive into Bynum, near Pittsboro, you'll realize why some folks call the place "Clydeville." Clyde's "critters"—chainsaw-hewn dogs, pigs, and reindeer, colorful fish, and penguin murals—seem to creep around everywhere.

Clyde's signature creations are the almost life-size animals he carves from roots, stumps, and logs and then outfits with body parts made of discarded items like old baseballs, tin cans, and plastic flowers. Many of his creations he slathers with bright paint, so the flock surrounding his house looks something like a rainbow zoo.

Jones, who was born in 1938, worked in a wood mill until he suffered a serious injury in 1979, when a log rolled on his leg and shattered a knee. As he healed, Jones went back to woodwork: Only this time, he was carving out creatures rather than boards. In the late 1980s he started painting as well, turning old doors and barren walls into canvases for garish yet folksy animal art.

Over time his yard filled up with the creatures, and neighbors starting asking for ones of their own. In fact, around Bynum, it's hard to find a piece of property where one of Clyde's carvings isn't prominently displayed.

Members of the folk-art zoo have traveled far and wide, having been displayed at art galleries and museums all over the world. But Clyde's biggest fans are doubtless the ones who live in the community his critters call home. In 2006 Pittsboro celebrated the fifth annual ClydeFest, which is held on a Saturday in April. It's a vibrant country arts fest, done in Clyde's eclectic, whimsical style: Kids act, dance, sing, paint, and create their own little masterworks with Clyde and other local artists. The festival winds up with Jones carving a new critter out of a cedar log; the sweet-smelling varmint is then auctioned, with the proceeds going to local nonprofit ChathamArts.

Clyde and Co. reside in the community of Bynum, off U.S. Highway 15/501 six miles south of Chapel Hill. Look for the CRITTER CROSSING sign and a yard bustling with wooden wonders. For the date and location of the next ClydeFest, contact ChathamArts at (919) 542–0394 or info@ chathamarts.org.

Clyde Jones, Bynum's critter-in-chief.

BLASTS FROM THE PAST

At first glance the land in and around Butner, about twenty minutes north of Durham, looks downright placid. Farms, grassy fields, and modest subdivisions dot the still largely rural landscape.

But just beneath the surface, Butner's got a potentially explosive problem that dates back to World War II. For much of the war, the town and its environs served as a 40,000-acre army training base. What kind of training? Artillery training.

Mortars, grenades, howitzer and bazooka shells. The big stuff and the small stuff. Some were just training rounds, with no explosive payload. But many of the munitions used on the base's fifteen bomb ranges were the genuine article, and to this day the community is still grappling with shells that hit the dirt generations ago.

That's because not all of the bombs exploded. In fact, thousands of items of unexploded ordnance—or UXO, in military shorthand—still lie just beneath flower beds, roads, and backyard basketball courts.

Miraculously, there has been only one injury, and no deaths, reported from the many mishaps with Camp Butner's leftover ordnance. But that doesn't ease the worries of many area residents. In 2001, for example, an eight-year-old raked up a live mortar round with the leaves in his yard.

The Army Corps of Engineers, which is responsible for cleaning up former military sites, is making a slow, steady effort to locate and remove Butner's UXO. But funding for the effort, the Corps admits, is insufficient, and, meanwhile, shell-shocked locals live with the uncertainty of just what they'll find next.

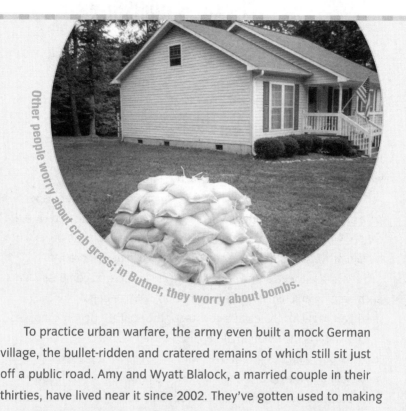

Other people worry about crab grass; in Butner, they worry about bombs.

To practice urban warfare, the army even built a mock German village, the bullet-ridden and cratered remains of which still sit just off a public road. Amy and Wyatt Blalock, a married couple in their thirties, have lived near it since 2002. They've gotten used to making unsettling discoveries on their property, including a detonator, a 155-mm white phosphorus shell, a live howitzer round, and enough shrapnel to fill a bucket.

Every time the Blacks come across a rusted explosive, the army dutifully sends the bomb squad from Fort Bragg to retrieve and dispose of it. After the most recent find—the howitzer round—a soldier from the squad carefully extracted it from creekside mud, gently scooped it into a metal tube, and then took it away for detonation at a nearby National Guard facility.

Watching the soldiers drive off, Wyatt sighed. "Maybe sooner or later we'll get 'em all," he said.

In the meantime, if you happen to come across one of Butner's time-worn explosives, no matter how decayed it looks, DO NOT TOUCH IT. Walk away on your tiptoes and call the authorities.

Sacred Spiral

Calvander

Just north of Carrboro, where the college-town neighborhoods give way to gently sloping fields, lies a sacred spiral.

From a distance it looks like a mini-Stonehenge. On closer inspection it's a circle of thirty boulders, 90 feet in diameter, that spiral toward the center, where a stone altar sits. On the altar a metal plaque bears a Navajo prayer about how the earth's beauty can be restored.

Four large stones at the edges of the circle serve as compass points, each bearing an animal-related inscription: a white buffalo for the north, an eagle for the east, a coyote for the south, a bear for the west.

The spiral is the creation of Carrboro-based architect and builder John Hartley, who designs houses with an eye toward preserving natural beauty and the natural environment—a principle he has followed since studying Native American philosophies about how to live in the

Save yourself a trip to Stonehenge—Calvander's got plenty to ponder.

world. He calls it "sacred ground," and indeed, it's a restful, pleasantly holy-feeling place. (Let your mind wander a bit, and it's easy to feel like you're in a scene from C. S. Lewis's *Narnia*.)

The spiral is located on Johns Woods Road, half a mile north of the intersection of Old Fayetteville and Hillsborough Roads, which is near Carrboro's town limit. You'll see it on a grassy knoll to the right. Please tread lightly—it's a sacred place.

Yappy Hour
Carrboro

"It was started on a dare," says Stacy Smith, founder of Wiener Dog Day—and, watching scores of dachshunds wriggle around the lawn of Weaver Street Market in Carrboro, it's easy to believe her.

It all began six years ago, when Smith and her husband were having a meal on one of the Market's picnic tables. As owners of a beloved wiener dog named Oscar Meyer, she says, "We thought it would be really funny to have a bunch of [dachshunds] dominate the lawn." Could she do it? The doggie die was cast.

And so it was that in 2002 she organized the first Wiener Dog Day, which puts any dachshund who shows up on center stage. Now scampering toward its sixth annual celebration, the event is held at the same location on the first or second Sunday in October (what with all the "wieners," the event is "kind of Oktoberfesty," Smith notes).

To the delight of onlookers (well, most of them anyway), the dogs have a busy afternoon. After a parade around the lawn, they compete to see who's got the best costume, who does the best trick, who can go lowest in a doggie-sized limbo contest, and who can best navigate a small obstacle course. Throughout the proceedings the humans do a lot of clapping and laughing, and the dogs raise a cacophony of yelps.

How many dogs show up to take pride in their unabashedly hot dog–like form? Although close to fifty seemed to be in attendance at the last Wiener Dog Day, the way they scrambled around, it was impossible to be sure. "I've been trying to count the dachshunds," Smith sighed. "It's like trying to count fish."

Over time the event has morphed into a fund-raiser for the North Carolina chapter of the nonprofit Dachshund Rescue of North America. For details, visit the organization's Web site at www.drna.org.

In Carrboro, every wiener dog has his day.

ONE HUNDRED COUNTIES—COUNT 'EM

Krissy Gray, a traveling nurse, was born in Gaston County, grew up in Jackson County, moved to Orange County fifteen years ago and then to neighboring Chatham County, and so on. We caught up with her during her time as an operating room nurse at UNC Hospitals in Chapel Hill.

Understandably, Gray has logged many a mile on North Carolina roads. For reasons she can't explain, every time she travels, she keeps a running tab of all the counties she passes through. So when someone at a Christmas party mentioned that North Carolina has one hundred of them, her ears perked up.

"One hundred," she thought. "That's a nice round number—kind of like having fifty states."

That nice round number packs some political potential, coming in handy for politicians trying to demonstrate their fealty to *all* of North Carolina. In 2002, for example, Senator John Edwards issued a press release titled "Edwards Visits All 100 Counties." Edwards, who had presidential aspirations, had been criticized by state Republicans for running off to too many foreign hot spots, Hollywood fund-raisers, and key primary states. Not to worry, the release seemed to say, Edwards had proven he's a homeboy by traveling "from Murphy (where he went to college) to Manteo (where he honored Andy Griffith)."

OK, so Edwards visited every county. But can he name them all? In alphabetical order? Gray can.

CONTINUED

Of course it took a little practice. "When somebody said there were one hundred, I thought I knew enough that I could nail them all," she says. She had an impromptu crack at it, but to her chagrin she could only list about thirty counties off the top of her head.

So Gray pulled out an atlas and spent a day memorizing. Her method? Learn a few at a time and then keep writing lists until they were all etched in her brain. "I got obsessed," she says. "I couldn't stop until I got them all right."

Gray learned a lot about her home state in the process. For example, the most common first letter for North Carolina counties is c, which starts fifteen of the names. M is the second most common, with eight. Of all of them, it's hard to pick a favorite, Gray says. Hers would probably be Transylvania, followed closely by Carteret, Currituck, and Duplin.

By New Year's Day following that fateful Christmas party, Gray was ready with her new party trick. A circle of friends looked on dumbstruck as she rattled off the North Carolina one hundred. Later, we asked her to do it again, and she nailed it.

John Edwards, if you're listening, here's an abridged version of what she said: "Alamance, Alexander, Alleghany, Anson, Ashe . . . Wayne, Wilkes, Wilson, Yadkin, Yancey."

Curiosities in the North Carolina Collection
Chapel Hill

The University of North Carolina–Chapel Hill's Wilson Library is revered by southern scholars as a repository of some of the most complete and revealing archival collections in the region. It also happens to house a remarkable assortment of historical oddities.

"There are some interesting things that you wouldn't think you'd find here," notes Linda Jacobson, assistant keeper of the library's North Carolina Collection Gallery. For example, the collection counts among its holdings a plaster copy of Napoleon Bonaparte's death mask, made by the late emperor's personal physician. Then there's a sizable collection of exotic stuffed animals—former residents of the university's now-defunct zoology museum.

Some of the items are quintessential state curiosities. Take the Chang and Eng Bunker display in the gallery, for instance. The most famous Siamese twins in history, the brothers spent the latter part of their lives in Mount Airy, where they each raised a sizable family. The display features extraordinary artifacts—most donated by the Bunkers' descendants—including the brothers' handwritten ledger kept while traveling the world, an embroidered birch bark card case presented to them in Quebec in 1835, an original watercolor portrait of the twins, yellowed promotional fliers from the brothers' public appearances, and a ceramic figurine of the two, circa 1830.

Many other unique corners of state history—from North Carolina's first gold mine to its first library, the 1,800-volume contents of which are on display—are explored in the permanent and rotating exhibits. The North Carolina Collection Gallery is located on Wilson Library's main floor. It's free and open to the public Monday through Friday, 9:00 A.M. to 5:00 P.M.; Saturday, 9:00 A.M. to 1:00 P.M.; and Sunday, 1:00 to 5:00 P.M. For information on the latest exhibits, call (919) 962–1172 or visit www.lib.unc.edu/ncc/gallery.html.

Positively Goole-ish
Chapel Hill

So, your name is Peter Dromgoole, and you're given to dramatic behaviors. Seems like you're destined for a strange history, at best.

And so it went for ol' Pete, who attended UNC–Chapel Hill, the country's oldest public university, in the 1830s. According to *North Carolina Legends,* which was published by the state's Division of Archives and History in 1980, Dromgoole was "a high-strung fellow, fond of gambling and drinking and horse racing," who also happened to be "aristocratic, proud, and defiant."

Such a youth was bound to find some trouble and leave a legacy. In 1833 he mysteriously disappeared and was never heard from again.

As it happened, he met his doom the night after he graduated, if the most widely circulated story is true. He's said to have wound up in a duel with a rival suitor for a lovely "Miss Fanny" and to have fallen that night from his opponent's bullet. Some say that his blood, which poured onto a gray rock, left stains that can still be seen today.

As for Fanny, the legend says she slid into a deep depression and died in short order from a broken heart. Peter's ghost and hers still meander about, according to the lore.

Paying homage to Dromgoole, in 1889, five students founded a secret society (or an awfully melodramatic fraternity, depending on whom you ask) called the Order of Dromgoole. They later changed their name to the Order of Gimghoul and, in the 1920s built Gimghoul Castle near campus to do what, exactly, no one seems to know for sure (though word of raucous parties occasionally seeps out through the structure's medieval rocks).

Today, as ever, the castle is in very private hands, but it's not too hard to catch a glimpse of it: To try, find your way to the end of Gimghoul Road on the eastern edge of the UNC–Chapel Hill campus and peek through the trees.

Go West, Young Fan

Charlotte

So you want to hold a festival focused on films from the American West—movies set in tumbleweed-laden deserts and frontier towns. Where better, then, to do that than in a state that's so far east it shores up to the Atlantic Ocean? And while you're at it, why not hold the festival in a city covered in glass and concrete—a city like Charlotte?

Unlikely as it may seem, the Western Film Fest, one of the largest of its kind, is hosted in a city better known for its bankers than its buckaroos.

How did the Queen City come to corral the festival? In short (so to speak), Wayne Short, an accountant with a yen for westerns, arranged for Charlotte to hold the first one in 1980. For a while the festival came and went intermittently, but now it's an annual affair.

The festival is chock-full of western film wonders, with daylong screenings (the term "B-western" is an accolade here), panel presentations, well-stocked vendors, and a posse of former cowboy and cowgirl actors from the genre's golden age—along with plenty of look-alikes. And then there's the festival's moment of glory—the presentation of the Ernest Tubb Memorial Award. Past winners include actor George Hamilton IV and the Statler Brothers, a country-and-western act.

The Western Film Fest is held every July and has been drawing some 500 fans of late. For details on seeing how the West was won, steer yourself to www.westernfilmfest.tripod.com.

The Other Hilton Sisters

Charlotte

Nowadays, Nicki and Paris Hilton are all the rage in the tabloids. Time was, another (and infinitely more interesting) pair of Hiltons had the spotlight. Born to a British barmaid and sold to the midwife who delivered them, Daisy and Violet Hilton (1908–1969) were conjoined twins who rode a roller coaster of a life together.

In their youth the sisters were physically abused and financially exploited by older relatives and displayed as circus freaks from the age of three on. At twenty-three they won their independence but kept on performing, mostly in the United States. They did vaudeville shows, Broadway musicals, and Hollywood films.

Although we haven't seen it, we're told that one of their main movies—*Chained for Life*—is excruciatingly bad. Still, one reviewer made it sound interesting enough, describing it as "a lurid tale in which one sister stands accused for murder, but questions are raised as to the fairness of sending her to jail if her innocent sister must go as well."

Despite their talent and resolve, the Hiltons' modicum of fame faded away as they aged. In the 1950s they ran a fruit stand in Florida. In the early 1960s they attempted a revival of sorts, showing up at drive-in theaters to promote reshowings of their movies.

And so it was that in 1962 they unexpectedly made a new (and final) home in Charlotte, where their agent abandoned them mid-tour. They found work at a local grocery store, where they weighed produce together until their death in 1969 at age sixty. The Hiltons rest where their remarkable journey left them—at the Queen City's Forest Lawn Cemetery.

The Naked Truth

Charlotte

Most of us own and occasionally wear clothes that make us uncomfortable—that funky polyester shirt, say, or that gut-crunching girdle. But a rarer breed would just prefer to wear no duds at all (weather permitting, we assume).

And while we're all free to strip down in the privacy of our homes, who do you turn to when you'd like to share your unclad bod with large groups of people? Why, to the North Carolina Naturists, of course.

"We are a group of individuals who enjoy a clothing-free lifestyle in the company of others who feel the same way," explains the club's information-packed Web site (www.ncnaturists.com). "Meetings and wholesome get-togethers are held at other members' homes as well as at area nudist resorts located in North and South Carolina."

If that doesn't sound so "wholesome," read on. "All overt sexual activity is . . . prohibited," the group insists. "Naturist clubs are family-oriented." Another important (and quite fitting, we would think) condition is the "two-towel" rule: "Polite nudist etiquette means that you always carry your own towel to sit or lounge on and a second one for the pool."

Intriguing as the group is, let's just say that neither of us could bare to visit with them in our, um, natural state. Fortunately, Jared Neumark, an intrepid reporter for the Charlotte newsweekly *Creative Loafing,* had the cojones to seek out the naked truth by attending one of the club's potluck picnics—and he followed the dress code.

The August 2006 get-together was attended by some twenty nudists. The only one with his clothes still on, Neumark's first order of business was going native. "I disrobed, then emerged from the bedroom with only my notepad," he recalled. "It crossed my mind to use my trusty journalism tool as a shield."

Trying to keep his eyes from wandering, Neumark started jotting down notes on the nude picnic scene. "The ratio of men to women is about four or five to one," he observed. "Not having gray hair is a rarity."

Neumark went on to observe that while the members shared a nude attitude, the similarities stopped there: "Naturists aren't aligned in social or political matters, and I was surprised when one NC Naturist told me most members are conservative." (Republican politicos take note: Here's a new demographic for you to target.)

Having let it all hang out since 1981, North Carolina Naturists is probably the oldest group of its kind in the state. There are at least two other Tarheel nude/naturist clubs—check the Raleigh and Outer Banks entries in this book for more about the people who prefer to wear less.

Keep on Truckin'
Cherryville

Grier Beam's first love was chickens, but poultry didn't pay the bills. Probably a good thing, too.

Beam grew up in a farm family of modest means and in the early 1930s went off to North Carolina State University in Raleigh to get a degree in poultry science. A foray into the egg business went bust, and, finding himself at home and in the midst of the Great Depression, Beam decided to take a different business tack.

He bought a 1931 Chevrolet truck on credit and set about hauling coal for the Lincoln County schools and transporting fresh-market produce north from Florida. His initial investment repaid itself handsomely, and within six years his wing-and-a-prayer trucking business was earning six figures.

Grier's Carolina Freight Carriers grew into one of the nation's biggest trucking companies and maintained its corporate headquarters here in Cherryville until 1995.

All the while, Grier spent his free moments collecting and restoring the trucks his business used through each phase of its spectacular growth, right down to the 1931 Chevrolet that got it all rolling. Today, they're housed in the C. Grier Beam Truck Museum, a study in shiny red paint and chrome grilles. In a fitting nod to history this 7,500-square-foot museum is linked to the gas station that housed Grier's first office.

The museum is located at 111 North Mountain Street in Cherryville. Call (704) 435–3072 or visit www.beamtruckmuseum.com for hours of operation.

Gnome Alone

Davidson

Depending on whom you ask, gnomes are either charming or creepy. They grace our gardens and have been the butt of many a practical joke. For Tom Clark the little guys are a labor of love.

Described as "the most prolific gnome sculptor in the country," Clark has crafted more than 1,000 of them. "I was anxious to do 1,000," he told *Creative Loafing*'s Jared Neumark in 2006. "That came and went. I don't believe I can do 2,000, but I'll just keep on going and see what happens."

Clark was raised in Elizabethtown and later went to school at Davidson College, where he became a professor. A choice selection of his works is on view at the Tom Clark Museum, at 131 North Main Street. Call (704) 892–9213 or visit www.cairnstudio.com for more information.

SHOOTIN' IN THE NEW YEAR

Come New Year's Eve, you can see and hear fireworks in the sky above thousands of American cities and towns. It's quite a spectacle, all right, but the folks in Cherryville might consider all that flash a little lackluster, compared to their "New Year's Shoot."

A tradition among some town residents for as long as anyone can remember, the event has changed little since it was started by German settlers in the 1800s. Every New Year's Eve, local shooting clubs gather their members for a little old-fashioned gunplay.

Make that *real* old-fashioned: Cherryville's shooters do their thing with vintage black-powder muskets—the sort that haven't seen much action since colonial days. In fact, the guns used today fire no projectiles, but they sure do raise a ruckus of sound and smoke.

On the night before January 1, teams of musket-bearing locals gather and go from house to house in certain neighborhoods, firing their guns at selected stops. The settlers, historians say, shot the muskets as both a good luck wish and a means of warding off evil spirits, witches, and the like.

Today, it's all done in good fun, but the "shoot-ins" do have their critics, especially after a 2005 tragedy in which one of the muskets exploded in the hands of an eighteen-year-old, killing him. In the aftermath, some seem determined to carry on the ear-splitting celebration—albeit with as much care as possible. "There's no effort in place here to end the practice," Cherryville mayor Bob Austell said.

"This is something that's been going on in Cherryville for more than 200 years. We have grandsons firing off muskets that once belonged to their grandfathers." Austell added that "perhaps it's a good time for us to highlight safety again and make sure every shooter has safety on their mind."

Back in the day, the shooters would preface their blasts with a speech that ended with these words:

We have this New Year's morning called you by your name

And disturbed you from by your rest.

And if it be your desire

Our guns and pistols they shall fire.

Since we hear of no defiance

You shall hear the art of science.

When we pull trigger and powder burns

You shall hear the roaring of guns.

Oh, daughters of righteousness, we will rise

And warm our eyes and bless our hearts,

For the old years gone and the New Year's come

And for good luck we'll fire out guns.

A Harrowing Experience

Denton

Hardly anyone threshes anymore. But time was, most anyone you met would've threshed once or twice in his or her life.

Wait—just what is threshing?

To thresh is to remove the seeds from grain—be it oats, wheat, barley, or rye—from the husks and straw. The job used to be done with a tool called a flail, but beginning in the nineteenth century, as farm technology leapt forward, automatic threshing machines began to make short work of a chore as old as agriculture itself.

Today's nostalgia for simpler, more pastoral times and, yes, even threshing reaches a fever pitch during the last weekend in June, when farm equipment enthusiasts sweep down on Denton, 30 miles south of Winston-Salem. The Old Thresher's Reunion bills itself as "the greatest steam, gas and antique farm machine show in the southeastern U.S," and it just might be that. According to the festival's organizers, exhibitors from all over the country tow in more than 1,000 restored antique gas tractors for the four-day event. Attendees can watch the nation's agricultural past belch, buck, whirl, and spin to life with gassy abandon.

But lest we forget the real origins of the term "horsepower," the Thresher's Reunion also features hundreds of draft horses and mules, demonstrating their knack for a host of farm activities, from threshing and shelling corn to plowing and harrowing.

The reunion is held at the Denton Farm Recreation Park, which, to be honest, is quite the attraction itself. If you weary of all the threshing, there are historic buildings to see, including an old country store, a U.S. post office, the old Jackson Hill Church, a radio museum, and log cabins. And it's hard to miss the Handy Dandy Railroad—an old-timey steam engine that runs circles 'round the forty-acre park.

For information on the Old Thresher's Reunion, call (800) 458–2755 or visit www.threshers.com. To get there from Winston-Salem, take Highway 52 to the Lexington exit; turn left and follow Highway 52 to Highway 64 East. Take Highway 64 East to Highway 109 and exit right at Skipper's Seafood. Follow Highway 109 South to Denton (approximately 9 miles). Turn right at the second stoplight in Denton and follow the signs to the park.

Tobacco Tribute
Durham

Sure, tobacky's wacky, causing cancer and all that. But it sure is the stuff of an interesting museum, especially when placed in the smoky heart of tobacco country.

Witness the Duke Homestead and Tobacco History Museum in north Durham, where the golden leaf (or "stinking weed," depending on your perspective) gets a loving treatment. Situated on several acres, the homestead offers a walking tour of well-maintained mainstays of tobacco history: a curing barn, a pack house, a reconstruction of the "first tobacco factory"—the corn crib where Washington Duke, the founding father of the tobacco industry, started manufacturing smoking tobacco in 1865.

For the curiosity-seeker, though, the real finds are inside the museum, which features informative displays on every stage of the tobacco production process. What's more, the place delves into some fascinating facets of tobacco culture.

There's a room full of mannequins operating tobacco cutters, packing machines, rolling machines, and the like. There's a "hall of fame" of tobacco's movers and shakers. A vintage 1950s living room setting offers visitors the chance to view TV ads from that period touting the product's good taste, supposed health benefits, and long-burning qualities. Another display surveys cheery tobacco ads that ran from the 1960s to the 1980s, before they were banned from most media. There's a lovely collection of pipes, from the corncob type to the ornately engraved Meerschaum variety, and a nice assortment of vintage cigarette machines and ashtrays.

One exhibit, "The Spitting Image: A History of Spittoons and Cuspidors," pays homage to smokeless tobacco, displaying scores of spit receptacles (they've all been thoroughly cleaned, we're happy to report).

As you proceed through the displays, the museum gets curiouser. Near the end is a wall depicting "the tobacco debate through the ages." Suffice it to say that tobacco's critics get short shrift in the Tobacco History Museum, but the display does offer a pointed 1601 comment from King James I, who judged smoking "a custom loathsome to the eye, hateful to the nose, harmful to the brain, dangerous to the lungs."

"Mr. Creepy" knows a thing or two about growing tobacco.

Across the room from King James's words of warning sits a tobacco tribute without rival: a full-scale replica of the Liberty Bell, made entirely of tobacco. "The bell contains enough tobacco to manufacture 150,000 cigarettes and weighs over 300 pounds," a plaque explains. "Over 200 hours of work by the art department of R.J. Reynolds Inc. was required to finish the bell."

As if all that weren't enough, the museum is also home to the famous life-size tobacco farmer automaton. Press a button, and he comes to life in a somewhat herky-jerky fashion to tell you how tobacco travels from seed to store. It's his performance, oddly enough, that seems to make the biggest impression on visitors.

Given his influence, we wondered what his name is. "I call him 'Mr. Creepy,'" one museum staffer said with a laugh. One of her colleagues protested. "He's the best employee we've got," he insisted. "He's always on time, he's always here."

Admission to the museum and homestead is free. For directions and hours, call (919) 477–5498 or visit www.duke homestead.nchistoricsites.org. If you can't make it there, check out the online tour at www.ibiblio.org/dukehome.

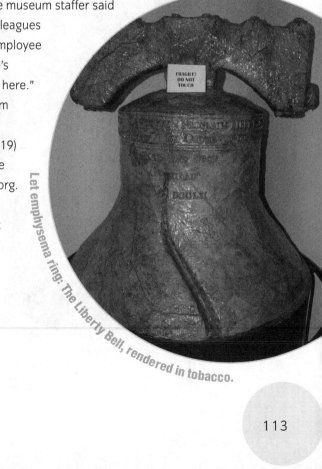

Let emphysema ring: The Liberty Bell, rendered in tobacco.

Fantasy Island
Durham

If the good Lord made a group of animals cuter than the lemurs, we don't want to know about it. With their big eyes, opposable thumbs, and taste for mischief, these distant relatives of monkeys, apes, and, yes, humans, put the a in "adorable."

Unfortunately, they also put the e in "endangered." On their home island of Madagascar, off the African coast, lemurs have their slender backs against the proverbial wall because of expanding slash-and-burn agriculture and that nation's burgeoning human population.

Jeepers, creepers, where do lemurs get their peepers?

While things look bad for lemurs in their home country, in Durham they're getting a bit of a reprieve. The Duke Lemur Center (until recently, the Duke Primate Center) was established in 1966 as a sanctuary for rare and endangered primates, including lemurs, tarsiers, lorises, and bushbabies. Sited on eighty-five acres within Duke Forest, the center is a home-away-from-home for roughly 250 of these primates, known in scientific circles as prosimians. The center's goals are study, conservation, and promoting biodiversity.

The Lemur Center is open to the public by appointment only. Visitors must be on a guided tour led by a staff member or docent. Tours can be arranged Monday through Saturday by calling (919) 489–3364. They book up early during the spring and summer months, so plan well in advance. For more information, visit www.lemur.duke.edu.

Top Brass
Durham

When was the last time you had your euphonium tuned up? If you don't have an answer, chances are it's time you paid a call to the Tuba Exchange Inc. This Durham business is world-renowned as a place where the biggest of brass instruments—tubas, euphoniums, sousaphones—come to be bought, sold, and restored to their former glory.

CEO Vince Simonetti founded the company in the early 1980s. A native of New Jersey, Simonetti has a lifelong passion for the tuba that took him around the country with a number of touring classical music outfits, notably the Martha Graham Dance Company and the Moisieff Ballet Company of Russia. In 1967 he moved to North Carolina to serve as principal tuba player with the North Carolina Symphony.

A career in a number of regional symphonies followed, but Simonetti was the sort of guy who just couldn't be kept in the orchestra pit, and a little more than a decade later he founded a repair and sales business catering strictly to the heavies of the brass world. In 1993 the company was incorporated as The Tuba Exchange Inc.

The tuba was developed during the nineteenth century to provide the necessary bass notes in symphonies and brass bands. The instrument's roots date back at least to the Renaissance period, when an instrument called the serpent filled a similar role in ensembles. Today, the largest model tuba, the E-flat, is fashioned from 16 feet of polished brass tube, turned in on itself like a coiled snake and set with valves that allow different notes to be sounded. Beyond its unmatched huffing, puffing, and flatulent timbre, a tuba is a feat of engineering.

If you're curious about tubas (and really, who isn't?), you might pay Simonetti and son (John Simonetti is the store's sales manager) a call

How low can you blow? Find out at the Tuba Exchange.

and feast your eyes on the company's collection of historic instruments, which includes a few specimens of the tuba's nineteenth century progenitor, the ophicleide. (Heck, if you're expecting, the store might be a good place to pick up some ideas for baby names.)

To reach the Tuba Exchange Inc., take Interstate 40 to exit 279A (Durham Freeway). Take Durham Freeway to exit 12C (Duke Street), stay left, and take your first left on Jackson Street. Follow Jackson to Vickers and continue on Vickers until the first light (Morehead Avenue). Turn right on Morehead until it crosses Chapel Hill Road. Turn left onto Chapel Hill Road and follow it 0.4 mile. For information, call (800) 493–8822. For more information, as well as a virtual tour of the company's historic collection, visit www.tubaexchange.com.

Parapsychology 101
Durham

Just as surely as many people are enchanted with extrasensory perception, telepathy, clairvoyance, and all manner of psychic phenomena, many others are ready to ridicule those who try to study these phenomena for real.

No matter—at least not at Durham's Rhine Research Center, an unabashed paranormal research center that's the finest of its kind in the world. At Rhine no one blanches at probing the farthest reaches of the human experience—even when those experiences seem like something out of the *Twilight Zone*.

The center's long, strange trip began in 1927, when Joseph and Louisa Rhine came to Duke University, where they quickly carved out a reputation as the country's top parapsychology researchers, producing serious studies from the fringe.

Joseph Rhine (1895–1980) made *ESP* a household word. Against the odds—and most of his colleagues in traditional science, as well—he probed and tried to prove the existence of various psychic phenomena. While the jury's still out on most of what he studied, it's fair to say that he set off a field of inquiry that continues to fascinate.

Today, the center is thriving, though no longer affiliated with Duke. It conducts ongoing research, publishes the *Journal of Parapsychology*, and hosts free public presentations on topics ranging from "ESP in Animals" to "How to Be More Psychic" to "What Do You Do When You See a Ghost?"

Rhine Research Center, at 2741 Campus Walk Avenue, Building 500, is open from 9:00 A.M. to 5:00 P.M. on weekdays. It won't hurt to call ahead, at (919) 309–4600, to tell them you're coming (though, as trained psychics, they probably know already). For plenty of paranormal history and the latest on Rhine's programs, visit www.rhine.org.

Edith Carter's Whippoorwill Academy and Village
Ferguson

Such was Edith Ferguson Carter's love for the story of Tom Dula (see Wilkesboro) that at one time she decided to do a few works of art depicting the life of the hanged man and his onetime girlfriend, Laura Foster. Forty-five paintings and drawings later, the Tom Dooley Art Museum was born. Carter's magnum opus is housed today in the loft of the Whippoorwill Academy, a one-room schoolhouse that Carter had disassembled nearby and rebuilt here in 1986.

As one might imagine, Carter's consuming passion for the Dula story went further than just artwork—over time she managed to collect Dula's original tombstone, his war records, the door handle to his home, and a lock of Foster's hair. They're here, and ready for your inspection.

The Whippoorwill Academy was built in 1880 by local miller Andy Gould. Its name derived from a local observation that "it was built so far back in the woods that not even the whippoorwills could find it." Members of the Dula and Foster family lines both were educated here over the years, as well as a onetime poet laureate of North Carolina.

Other buildings at the "village" include a two-room country store, built in the 1940s using lumber from a devastating flood. There is a replica of the cabin Daniel Boone and his family lived in during the 1760s. There is a log smokehouse built of eighteenth-century materials and, nearby, a newly constructed Chapel of Peace (available for weddings).

Carter is irrepressible. Her village currently includes eleven buildings, and a Beaver Creek Forge and a Weaving Shed are also planned for the location. Her Whippoorwill Academy and Village are open to the public Saturday and Sunday from 3:00 to 5:00 P.M. and weekdays by appointment. The site is closed January through March except by appointment. From Wilkesboro, follow signs for the W. Kerr Scott Dam and Reservoir to Highway 268 West. After traveling 2.5 miles on Highway 268, turn right at signs for the reservoir's Visitor Assistance Center.

Admission is free, but donations are accepted and appreciated. To arrange a visit, call (336) 973–3237. If a visit here doesn't quite give you a Dula fix, the hanged man's homesite and grave are located a mile from the Whippoorwill Academy on Tom Dooley Road, overlooking the Yadkin River. Laura Foster is buried about 5 miles away in Happy Valley, Caldwell County, on Highway 268.

A Thirst for History
Granite Falls

Alan Huffman's business is totally liquid. Which is to say that the Antiquities Vending Company, which he started in 1989, is pretty much the first and last drop when it comes to soda machine history. Name your favorite soda, and think about the machine that dispensed it for you, and odds are he could re-create the experience for you with the pop of a cap.

Huffman runs what he calls "a protective habitat for endangered soda machines." He's collected more than 1,000 of them and displays restored versions of some 400 at his Soda Machine Museum in Granite Falls. If you arrange a visit, he'll walk you through rows and rows of pop dispensers. "This is the first soda machine in the history of the world,"

Alan Huffman never met a soda machine he didn't like.

he says, pointing to a squat model made in Atlanta in 1925. "I've got number two too." Later, we learned that he just happens to have number three as well.

He's also got the fastest drink dispenser on record, the first one to pour soda into cups, the first refrigerated model, the first upright one, the first can vendor, Coke's first, Pepsi's first, and Orange Crush's first, among many others. Some of the machines are the only remaining models on the planet, and he's still collecting rare ones. Huffman's thirst for soda history, it seems, will never be quenched.

His company has made its mark refurbishing and marketing vintage soda machines and replicas. But it's clear that at heart he's really an insatiable collector—the kind who's willing to share what he finds. He opened the museum in 2006, along with an adjoining event space, Club Cola, and he's got plans to expand the facility to include vintage department store displays and other relics of modern Americana. His soda museum, we should note, is also home to lovingly restored 1950s televisions, radios, washers, and jukeboxes.

So what's Huffman's favorite soda? His answer is most unexpected: "Actually, my favorite soda is either water or Arizona Iced Tea," he says.

The Soda Machine Museum and Club Cola are located at 30 South Main Street. To arrange a visit, log on to www.antiquevending.com for contact information.

Odds and Ends
Greensboro

The Greensboro Historical Museum, founded in 1924, pays tribute to highlights of the city's history. Some of the holdings might seem somewhat mundane, unless you're a curiosity-seeker.

If you are, this free museum operated by the city of Greensboro has some wonders awaiting you. Among the more unique items preserved here are:

- Rare relics from the life of famed short story writer O. Henry, including his baby cradle, one of his top hats, and some of his letters, draft writings, and sketches.

- Prized possessions of North Carolina native Dolley Madison (wife of James Madison, of founding father fame), including some of her trend-setting turban hats.

- The late Robert and Capelia McKinney's one-of-a-kind collection of historic American glass objects.

The museum, which is located downtown at the intersection of Summit Avenue and Lindsay Street, is open from 10:00 A.M. to 5:00 P.M., Tuesday through Saturday, and from 2:00 to 5:00 P.M. on Sunday (except on official holidays). For more information, call (336) 373–2043 or visit www.greensborohistory.org.

He's Got Legs (and He Knows How to Use Them)
Henderson

One man's art is another man's smut—and if you don't believe it, take a gander at Ricky Pearce's sizable sculpture.

His concrete rendering of a pair of female legs, which jut out 40 feet in length and rise 17 feet at the knees (weighing some 40,000 pounds each), is a piece of public art without parallel. It's lovingly landscaped, with a crop of neatly pruned bushes and trees at the area where the legs part. It's lit up at night, and one giant thigh sports a garter belt. In front of it all is a metal trellis bearing the word "Reminiscing." Across the street from the legs, Pearce has installed a giant-size pair of high-heeled shoes.

The sculpture sits where you might least expect it—in a stretch of rural road not far south of the Virginia border. Upon seeing it, you just have to ask yourself, "What the hell is going on here?"

Thigh-master Ricky Pearce wants you to see his legs.

Ask Pearce, who runs a backhoe company and spent three years building the leggy landmark, and he's happy to explain. One day about five years ago, the sculptor says, he got inspired while gazing around his office. "I had a picture of Marilyn Monroe on my desk," he recalls, and all of a sudden, just looking wasn't enough. "I told my friend, 'Well, I'm going to do a sculpture of these legs.'"

The piece of audacious art has prompted a small share of complaints from some neighbors, but others have come to view it with something like pride. "I think it's like anything else," Pearce says. "You get those that like it, and those that don't like it. . . . I don't have to go along with their beliefs, and they don't have to go along with mine."

Through the minor controversies Pearce has welcomed the publicity they've brought to his sculpture. "If you don't have critics, you don't have any advertising," he says.

Meanwhile, Pearce's legs have become a just-off-the-beaten-path attraction. "I have a lot of people come by to take pictures," he says. "One day, a whole baseball team came out from Raleigh." In fact, no less than singing superstar Tina Turner, who knows a thing or two about great legs, has stopped by for a visit.

"I see millionaires around here, who live not far from me, and they've got nice rock wall entrance columns," Pearce observes. "They're pretty—but they don't get as much attention as these legs do."

Pearce's legs are located at 525 Welcome Avenue in Henderson. They're always open.

Animal Farm

Hiddenite

For a number of years, Robbie and Carlton Crouch raised mainly donkeys on their hundred-acre farm, and miniature ones at that. And while they insist that small asses will always have a place at Lawzyday Farm, their list of livestock has grown over the years to include lemurs, bushbabies, coatimundis, phlangers, Siberian chipmunks, African crested porcupines, LaPerm cats, chinchillas, and hedgehogs, to name a very few of the species on display here. The Crouches, it seems, just can't help themselves around animals.

If mammals aren't your cup of tea, there is Millie, a gigantic fifty-pound spurred tortoise, all bedroom eyes and slow moves, as well as several other exotic reptiles. And if feathers are your thing, you'll be pleased to know that the Crouches also keep an aviary full of exotic birds.

Lawzyday Farm is open for guests by appointment only. Contact the Crouches at (704) 585–2113, or visit www.lawzydayfarm.com for a full report. The farm is located 1 mile east of Highway 90 south of Hiddenite.

Well Hello, Dollies

High Point

Angela Peterson had a thing for dolls. Her passion began with crèche dolls, the ceramic figures that depict the who's who of Christ's nativity—wise men, sheep, and the like. But Peterson soon cast her nets wider, and by the time she retired from a teaching career in 1977, she owned more than 1,000 dolls of every imaginable stripe. A few years later, she traded her collection to a retirement complex in exchange for perpetual accommodation.

Since Peterson's death, the collection has been on display at the Furniture Discovery Center. The dolls, dollhouses, doll costumes, and related items now number more than 2,500 and include more than 115 Shirley Temple dolls (!) and 17 figurines depicting notable African Americans. A Shadow Box Room contains a 6-foot mobile home in miniature.

The Angela Peterson Doll & Miniature Museum is located at 101 West Green Drive. Call (336) 885–3655 or visit www.highpoint.org for information.

Among the wonders at the Angela Peterson Doll & Miniature Museum.

126

Seeing the Forest

High Point

Talking trees are not just some fanciful imagining of the English author J. R. R. Tolkien. At High Point's Furniture Discovery Center, visitors can get a lecture from a leafy know-it-all.

High Point makes a fine point of its importance in the global furniture trade, but all those raw materials had to come from somewhere. The forest, namely. So maybe it's right that a tree should tell the story of where all the varieties of wood used in the home interiors trade come from. Or maybe it's just kind of creepy.

Beyond the virtual tree distinction, the Furniture Discovery Center is the nation's only museum of furniture design and manufacture and features displays on how everything from highboys to chairs are assembled and finished.

The museum is located at 101 West Green Drive in High Point. It's open Monday through Friday 10:00 A.M. to 5:00 P.M., Saturday 9:00 A.M. to 5:00 P.M., and Sunday 11:00 A.M. to 5:00 P.M. Call (336) 887–3876 for additional information, including admission prices.

Socks of Ages
High Point

Pam Stern doesn't mind people staring at her chest. In fact, she wishes more people would. Stern's chest, since you asked, is 36 feet tall and made of a composite material patterned to look like hardwood. A pair of 6-foot-long socks—one plain, one argyle—dangles from it. The 4-foot-wide, gold-leaf drawer pulls bolted to it glint in the sunlight.

In 2006 Stern bought the chest from the High Point Jaycees, which owned the city landmark for years. The wood-grained eminence is actually the home furnishing capital's second giant lowboy; the first was built in 1925 at the prompting of Frank Sizemore Sr., then executive secretary of the High Point Chamber of Commerce. Sited downtown at Church and North Main Streets, the so-called "bureau of information"

High Point's still looking for a man big enough to wear these socks.

served as the organization's offices until the early 1950s, when the Chamber donated it to the Jaycees, who later moved it to the present location and added office space to the back.

Today, the chest stands twice as tall as the original, which, incidentally, is still there, entombed inside the brown foam facade.

The chest has garnered national attention. It once appeared in a "Ripley's Believe It or Not" column, and a special edition Kentucky bourbon, bottled in glass shaped like the chest, sold out immediately upon its release in 1978. The city's steady stream of furniture buyers, both foreign and domestic, go out of their way to gawk at it.

Beginning in 1996, the chest received a total makeover and augmentation, overseen by the late architect and furniture designer Sidney Arthur Lenger. Its colonial-style outsides were modeled after a Goddard-Townsend block front chest built by the Harden Furniture Company, which is now on permanent display in the Visitor Information Center lobby of the High Point Convention & Visitors Bureau.

"Fifty years from now, we won't feel the need to redo the face again because it's a classic," Lenger said. "It will stand the test of time. It will stand as a true work of art because High Point deserves it, and the people of High Point deserve it." Huzzah!

The chest is located at 508 North Hamilton Street, at the intersection of Hamilton and Westwood in downtown High Point. For more information, contact the Convention and Visitors Bureau at (336) 884–5255.

Trane Station
High Point

The statue of jazz great John Coltrane that stands at the corner of South Hamilton and Commerce Streets is lifelike and beautifully proportioned, ably conveying the purpose and creative intensity for which the late saxophonist was known. And yet for some reason, people seem to pay the most attention to the man's feet.

"People say that his shoes, especially, look real," says Joanna Easter, describing the 8-foot-tall statue she helped bring to the city's downtown in September 2006.

Coltrane, who collaborated with Miles Davis and fellow North Carolinian Thelonious Monk before going on to form a long-standing quartet, was born in Hamlet, North Carolina, and moved with his family to High Point when he was three years old. He lived here until he graduated from high school and began military service. The quiet, earnest musician lived on nearby Underhill Street and learned his first chops in the school band. According to Easter, it was about time to bring the city's most celebrated native son home.

"I serve on the downtown improvement committee, and we've done a few things downtown—typical urban planning stuff, you know. Well, we started thinking we needed to put up some statues down here, but I said *please,* we've got to stop short of putting up a horse and a fountain. I thought we could do better than that."

The effort took three years and roughly $100,000 to come to fruition, but the bronze likeness of Trane sculpted by former North Carolinian Thomas Jay Warren—complete with sax and dapper dress, right down to a "silk" ascot—has brought a giant to life in a place that doubtless had a formative impact on him.

"People who knew John Coltrane always talked about how his closest friends tended to be from the South—Monk, and Dizzy Gillespie, and others—so it just seems appropriate," Easter says.

But for now you'll have to excuse her. She's got some listening to do.

"Whenever I'm working late, I put on *Kind of Blue*," she says, referring to the best-selling Miles Davis album that features Coltrane. "You know what? It just doesn't get any better than that."

Jazz great John Coltrane gets his due in his once-hometown of High Point.

It Took a Village

Hillsborough

If you travel around these great United States, you can find plenty of attempts to romanticize the Native American populations that once ran the joint. There are vivid multimedia displays, ornate monuments, and elaborate outdoor dramas.

The Occoneechee Indian Village in Hillsborough takes a decidedly more understated approach. It's about as bare bones as Native American re-creations go, and it's all the more charming—and perhaps more genuine—for it.

Who needs teepees? Not the Occoneechee.

THE PIEDMONT

No bells and whistles here. Visitors park in a nearby municipal lot and then take a short trek to the village, which sits, with no fanfare, a few hundred yards from sometimes-bustling downtown Hillsborough.

Our visit found the village surrounded by a cordon of orange mesh fencing, an oddly modern accoutrement that made the place look a bit like one of modern artist Christo's large-scale installations. (The plastic fencing, as it happens, is there to keep visitors from traipsing into the unique, streamside ecosystem that surrounds the village.)

A walk around the fence takes you into the village, which is encircled by 10-foot-high wooden posts that are sharpened at the top. Inside, it's a basic but somewhat surreal environment, especially when it's as empty as it was the afternoon we ventured in. The village features a communal fire area, some crude wooden structures, and a number of thatch huts built to resemble the Occoneechee's seventeenth century housing units.

Visiting the village is a free, albeit no-frills, treat for history buffs. To get there, take Churton Street north into Hillsborough and turn right on Margaret Lane and then right on Cameron Street. Find a spot in the second parking lot on the right and then walk a few hundred feet toward town and to the left. When you see the orange fencing and empty huts, you're in Occoneechee territory.

What's in Your Drawers?

Jamestown

The late furniture designer Sidney Lenger had already given the World's Largest Chest of Drawers (see High Point) a significant upgrade. What was left? Why, how about building the World's Largest Highboy to match? He did, and the result today is an integral part of Furnitureland South's vast retail "campus."

The 85-foot-high landmark was built of steel framing overlaid with foam sheathing. A 6-foot finial sits atop the highboy, which is painted with a flamed wood-grain finish and set with golden drawer pulls. Scrolls near the chest's top are elaborately carved.

Furnitureland South is located off Business Road 85S in Jamestown (Interstate 85, exit 118), 2 miles on the right at 5635 Riverdale Drive. Call (336) 841–4328 or visit www.furniturelandsouth.com for details. But be careful: You may just leave with a houseful of new furnishings.

The Underground Railroad on Wheels

Jamestown

When the Civil War erupted, North Carolina officially fell in with the Confederates. But throughout the war the state's population proved—as it does to this day—that not everyone who lives here thinks the same way. Some eastern counties were in federal control through most of the war, and both the Piedmont and the mountain areas were strewn with Union sympathizers and opponents of slavery.

Wherever they lived, North Carolina's Quakers were some of the state's most committed abolitionists. And they proved their fealty to fighting human bondage long before the Civil War came along. For proof, witness the wagon preserved at Mendenhall Plantation.

At first glance the horse-drawn vehicle looks pretty standard, like a set piece from *Little House on the Prairie.* But if you go around back and look in the hidden compartment—a false-bottom space large enough to hold at least two people, and more if circumstances called for it—you'll see that this cart was built to carry a clandestine cargo.

The cargo was people on the great escape route known as the Underground Railroad, a loose-knit, exceedingly dangerous route that carried African Americans to free states. If caught, the escaped slaves faced a return to more bondage, the whip, or execution. Their white accomplices wouldn't fare so well, either.

Two Quaker boys from North Carolina were among those who, called by conscience, decided to run the gauntlet. Andrew Murrow (1820–1908) and Isaac Stanley (1832–1927), orphans raised by foster parents Joshua and Abigail Stanley, shuttled runaway slaves from North Carolina to Ohio during several trips on the wagon.

Each year, some 5,000 people visit Mendenhall Plantation, a well-preserved Quaker homestead on Jamestown's Main Street, to see the fabled wagon and other relics of "the other South." The site is open Tuesday through Sunday, with varying hours. Admission is $2.00 for adults and $1.00 for seniors, students, and children. Call (336) 454–3819 or visit www.mendenhallplantation.org for more information.

The Folly of It All

Kernersville

Jule Gilmer Korner (1851–1924) was the grandson of Joseph Korner, the uber-entrepreneurial German immigrant who founded Kernersville. Joseph may have gotten the town off the ground, but it was Jule—a noted art, design, and advertising expert—who gave the town a fun-house of the first order.

As he was building his extraordinary Victorian dwelling in the 1880s,

HOLEY TOMBSTONES

The wave of German immigrants who helped settle the Piedmont in the 1800s left a subtle legacy, which is to say that they adapted and assimilated pretty quickly, but also wove their culture into the multifaceted one that's rooted in North Carolina to this day.

If you look closely and in the right places, you'll see lasting markers of the unique talents and styles they brought from their homeland to the Tar Heel State. In Davidson County, in particular, there are many reminders of North Carolina's German settlers.

Many of them are in cemeteries, where visitors can witness a form of tombstone art in a concentration that might be unmatched in the United States. The tombstones were products of immigrant artisans who were trained and inspired by the Swisegood School, which was named after master cabinetmaker John Swisegood, a nineteenth-century German American. The most distinctive trait of the stones, which are made of North Carolina sandstone, are the graceful, simple German folk symbols—hearts, stars, and the like—that are carved out of them.

Today, the stones look something like carefully carved gray and dark green jack-o'-lanterns funneling fractured sunlight. They're something to see, especially at sunrise or sunset.

To find out how to have a gander at the holey tombstones, which are situated in several cemeteries, call the Davidson County Historical Museum at (336) 242–2035 or visit www.co.davidson.nc.us/museum.

one local passerby was heard to predict, "That will surely be Jule Korner's Folly." Korner liked the way that sounded, so he appropriated the slight and had "Korner's Folly" tiled above the house's entryway.

Today, Korner's Folly is maintained much as it was back then. The house sports twenty-two rooms, which are put together in something of an architectural jigsaw puzzle. The three-story building has seven levels, and the hallways and staircases snake about in an odd way that causes many a visitor to wonder where, exactly, he or she is heading. A number of secret passages and trap doors add to the house's aura of whimsical disorientation.

Korner's Folly also boasts fifteen fireplaces (one of which, a small one on the front porch, was installed to keep witches out), splendid woodwork, murals by German master Caesar Milch, an eclectic assortment of period artwork, a ballroom, and a fireproof smoking room made of marble and tile. The top floor holds a real delight: "Cupid's Park," the first private little theater in the nation. Today, this stunningly angled, mural- and fresco-covered room hosts productions by the Kernersville Little Theatre, which uses local amateur actors to produce a range of plays.

All the angles: The theater at Korner's Folly.

Korner's Folly is located at 412 South Main Street. It's open for public visits during limited hours on Thursday, Saturday, and Sunday. For the latest information on hours, admission fees, and special events, call (336) 996–7922.

Mr. UFO

Lincolnton

The truth is out there, and George Fawcett thinks he's found it—or at least as much of it as an avid UFO researcher can discover in sixty-odd years of investigating.

A devoted "ufologist," Fawcett has chased this otherworldly mystery with singular dedication. He first heard about the phenomenon during World War II, when U.S. Army Air Force pilots returned reports of strange aerial occurrences. Then, in 1951, he had a close encounter of his own while attending Lynchburg College in Virginia. Strolling across campus one morning, he saw what he describes as an orange-colored "disk-shaped object" hovering an estimated 300 feet above the ground.

"This persuaded me pretty quickly that there was something to UFO sightings," he later recalled. It was the last one he ever saw, but it was enough to launch a lifelong obsession.

A Mount Airy native and longtime Lincolnton resident, Fawcett can justly be called the dean of North Carolina ufology. He has researched more than 1,200 sightings, written several books and more than 1,000 articles on the subject, and founded numerous research groups, including the Tar Heel UFO Study Group and the North Carolina Chapter of the Mutual UFO Network, an international organization. To top it all off, Fawcett is one of few ufologists to make inroads to higher education, having taught a course—UFOs: A New Frontier of Science—from 1979 to 1982 at the Lincoln County Campus of Gaston College.

Known to his friends as "Mr. UFO," Fawcett, now in his late seventies, still keeps his eyes peeled for what lies beyond. He has spent the past few years continuing his research and lobbying for a North Carolina UFO museum, which he thinks might well be situated in nearby Charlotte.

For all his work in the past, Fawcett will likely be part of studies that will stretch far into the future. In 1998 he donated his voluminous research materials—the "Sauceriana Collection," he calls it—to the International UFO Museum in Roswell, New Mexico, home to the country's most publicized UFO incident.

Have you seen something unexplainable in the North Carolina skies? If so, history will thank you if you share it with Mr. UFO. Write him at 602 Battleground Road, Lincolnton, NC 28092.

Pucker Up
Louisburg

Darrell Williams couldn't have known how he would change the world when he decided to whistle instead of sing.

Williams, a Durham native, was a competitor at the Louisburg College Folk Festival in 1974. When it came time for him to sing a tune he had written called "Little River Blues," he opted instead to purse his lips and give a little whistle. It sounded pretty darn good, and *voilà*, the International Whistlers Convention was born.

Of course a festival doesn't become "international" overnight, and for a few years the whistlers' competitions that followed were modest affairs, held under a big shade oak on the school's campus. But in time it caught media attention, and crowds began to swell. In 1980 organizer Allen de Hart renamed the event the National Whistlers Convention. In time the "international" designation was added when it became clear that the affair had no boundaries; whistlers, and winning ones at that, were coming from as far away as England, Australia, and Japan.

The year 2005 will be remembered as the festival's "capacity year," when whistlers were so numerous (and from so many places: China, Japan, Thailand, India, Brazil, the Netherlands, Spain, Germany, Italy, Mexico, and thirty-two of the fifty United States) that the Franklin County Arts Council decided it needed to revamp the schedule and expand facilities to accommodate both the myriad performers and the fans of good whistling. And these folks ain't just whistling "Dixie": Winning tunes at the 2005 event included such highbrow selections as "Fête de la Belle," "Concerto in C Major," and the "Queen of the Night Revenge Aria." Try *that* at home.

Louisburg College, it must be mentioned, is also home to the world's largest collection of recorded whistling. Melodic mouth-music is so beloved in these parts that North Carolina governor Mike Easley designated the week coinciding with the festival "Happy Whistlers Week." Smiles and puckers all around.

Better plan ahead if you want to get a seat. The event takes place each April. For more information, visit www.whistlingiwc.com or contact the Franklin County Arts Council at artsfcac@nc.rr.com.

Mild, Mild West
Love Valley

When Charlotte native Andy Barker was fighting overseas during World War II, he daydreamed about creating a western-style town with Christian values back home in North Carolina, a place where a guy could saddle up and clip-clop along Appalachian foothills. He returned, worked in the construction business for a while, and, in 1954, spent his earnings on a piece of property in northwest Iredell County, where Love Valley stands today.

Now in his eighties, Barker remains the town's mayor and proprietor of Andy's Hardware, located along the town's 2-block dirt and manure Main Street. Within the town limits travel is limited to foot and horseback. Cars, you see, are barred from Love Valley.

It might be tempting to write the place off as a bit of wishful kitsch, but the modest burg, with its weathered wood facades, saloons, and handful of retro dwelling places, has been incorporated since 1963. A rock festival in 1970, featuring the Allman Brothers, paid for water and sewer improvements. Along with Mayor Barker, Love Valley has five councilmen. More than one hundred people actually live here, and on weekends and during special events the amount of cowboy hats and crinoline swells considerably.

Main Street's businesses, including the popular (not to mention only) watering holes Jack's Place and the Silver Spur Saloon, are open from Friday to Sunday afternoon only, but horse rentals and campground space are available all week long. There are regular rodeo events held here, and Love Valley's miles of equestrian trails are open year-round, except during deer season, when they are closed on weekdays.

Don't expect any gunfights or rowdy bordellos here; outside of a spooked horse, the gravest bodily threat posed by Love Valley is probably the aftermath of the town's annual chili cook-off.

A visit to Love Valley is free. Leave your car at the parking lot outside the town's main gate and saunter back to a simpler time. Visit www.lovevalley.com for information about a visit. From I–40 near Statesville, take exit 150 (Highway 115) and head north toward Wilkesboro. Make a slight left onto Mountain View Road. Turn right onto Love Valley Road.

Animal Kingdom
Mooresville

Raising strange animals has always been a family affair for Wendy Wilson. Her father, Henry Hampton, took an interest in exotic animals in the early 1970s and by 1993 had opened Lazy 5 Ranch. Wendy was sixteen years old at the time. Whereas most parents and children bond by, say, going to the mall together, or getting lunch at McDonalds, the Hamptons came together by bottle-feeding baby lemurs and mixing food for water buffaloes.

"I was raised with it," Wilson says. Her sister is a veterinarian, and her brother-in-law is a zookeeper with twenty-five years of experience under his belt.

By following the ranch's 3.5-mile loop road, visitors can take in the sight of nearly 750 animals from six continents without leaving the comfort of their cars. Some animals even approach the cars and look inside quizzically.

"Everyone's always asking me, 'What's your most exotic animal?'" says Wilson. "Well, we've got buffaloes, llamas, camels, a rhino, all kinds of antelopes and goats and nondomestic sheep, and birds, too: ostriches, emus, rheas, macaws, cockatoos. . . ." Nevertheless, she adds, "People love the giraffes," of which there are five.

This year the 180-acre ranch will see roughly 180,000 visitors, about half of them schoolchildren. The ranch is open in every season, and special events include a live nativity scene for the Christmas holiday. Guided wagon tours of the grounds are also available, including romantic twilight excursions for couples.

Admission is $8.50 for adults, $5.50 for children ages two to eleven, and $5.50 for seniors sixty and up. Lazy 5 Ranch is located on Highway 150 between Salisbury and Mooresville. Call (704) 663–5100 or visit www.lazy5ranch.com for more information.

From Bad to Worse

Morganton/Kona

The first person to have a look inside Charlie and Frances "Frankie" Silver's cabin after the fateful night of December 22, 1831, found shards of bone and greasy ashes inside the fireplace and, under the floorboards, a pool of blood "as big as a hog liver."

We may never know why the teenage bride killed her young husband or, moreover, why she killed him with an ax and then tried to burn his remains, but the story of the murder that took place in the tiny Mitchell County settlement of Kona refuses to go away. It lives on in ballads, ballets, plays, and scores of books, pamphlets, and magazine accounts.

Much of what comes down to us is conjecture, but even the unadorned story has all the elements of a saga: After murdering her husband and being found out, Frankie Silver hid from the law, was arrested and imprisoned, and eventually managed to escape with the help of family members. She was retrieved, tried, retried, and finally, on July 12, 1833, hanged at the Burke County seat of Morganton. The tale has so much apocryphal detail swirling around it that it's hard to know just what happened, but it's said that when Frankie was asked at the gallows if she had any last words, her father made a zipped-lips sign and shouted, "Die with it in ye, Frankie." Way to go, dad.

The job of hauling Frankie's remains home from Morganton was an unpleasant enough task, but worse given the time of year—summer—and the plodding means of transportation: horse-drawn wagon. By the by, Frankie's body began to decompose, and her father, thinking better of completing the macabre homecoming, buried her remains close to Morganton, near Buckhorn Tavern.

A granite marker put there in the 1950s marks the spot today, with a typo, no less: FRANKIE SILVERS—ONLY WOMAN EVER HANGED IN BURKE COUNTY. It is located on Buckhorn Tavern Road, off Highway 126, north of Morganton, on private property.

Charlie Silver's grave can be found at the Kona Baptist Church in Mitchell County. To get there, take U.S. Highway 19E to Highway 80 and follow it to Old Kona Road. The church is on the right. Silver's descendants maintain the Silver Family Museum inside the church. It's open during select times each summer. For more information, call the Mitchell County Chamber of Commerce at (828) 765–9483.

Where Andy Walked

Mount Airy

There is a certain kind of person who insists that the world of the *Andy Griffith Show*—a place of kindly sheriffs and bumbling deputies, simple lessons, honesty, and home-cooked meals—must exist somewhere. The show's leading man has always insisted otherwise, that the Mayberry of TV fame was not one place, but in fact a pastiche of southern towns.

Nevertheless, the faithful flock to Griffith's hometown, Mount Airy, looking for at least a reflection of that rustic world. And who are the citizens of Mount Airy to get in the way of a little good-natured delusion? Thus you have a town with an honest-to-God Floyd's Barbershop, an Aunt Bea's Restaurant, and a dead ringer for Barney Fife who shows up to promote the place on brochures and TV spots.

Today, Griffith spends most of his time on the Outer Banks, but the world's biggest collection of Griffith memorabilia remains in Mount Airy, thanks to the tireless work of one of the actor's schoolmates. Emmett Forrest spent three decades gathering Griffith ephemera before moving into a condominium and needing to find a place for all of it. Today, the collection has carved out a corner of the Main Oak Emporium in downtown and includes artifacts as rare as the suit Griffith wore on his latter-day TV drama *Matlock* and a plastic wrapper that once encased a pound or so of Andy Griffith Whole Hog Sausage, one of a line of food products put out during the zenith of the native son's celebrity.

If you happen to work up an appetite gazing on such wonders, treat yourself to a pork chop sandwich at Snappy Lunch, where a patented auto-tenderizer makes sure every sandwich tastes as good as the last.

The Main Oak Emporium has entrances along Main, Oak, and City Hall Streets in downtown Mount Airy. Call (336) 789–2404 for more information.

Working stiff: Sheriff Taylor never tires of greeting visitors.

Stuff It

Mount Pleasant

If you're reading this book, you're probably an American (though it's cool if you're not). If you're an American, you probably love accumulating stuff (though it's cool if you don't). Whoever you are, you can probably find something you want at Don Cline's shop, Cline's Country Antiques.

Located in a rural setting near Mount Pleasant, the place is a lusciously stocked junkyard of sorts. It's a nexus where things you don't quite want and things you want sit side by side.

Old store and company signs, oil-drum chicken sculptures, vintage Coke bottles, quirky old furniture, prosthetic limbs—you want it, you got it.

Cline's Country Antiques is located at 11839 Highway 49. For hours call (704) 436–6824.

It's the Water

Mount Vernon Springs

We had Mount Vernon Springs to ourselves the day we visited the historic site, located along a country lane not far from Siler City. A catbird mewed lazily from the woods nearby. No wasps stirred from the abundant nests on the moss-covered shelter above us. We walked down to the shallow cement foundation, bending close to the two pipes that jutted from it, burbling forth their steady stream of water. We knelt with all the solemnity of pilgrims to a holy site, like a pair of postmodern Ponce de Leóns.

We filled an empty Coke can. We tasted the water. It was soft on the tongue and had a faint bouquet of rotten egg. "Behold," we silently wondered, "is this the secret to health and beauty?"

Health and beauty flow for free at Mount Vernon Springs. Cups are not provided.

Apparently, somebody once thought so. Since the early 1830s the water that drips from the twin pipes at Mount Vernon, with their hopeful names—"Health" and "Beauty"—has been revered for its tonic properties.

Much is made today of the importance of staying "hydrated," but in the days before hospitals and HMOs, water from various springs was accorded health-giving powers that verged on the mystical.

These springs were discovered by settlers in the 1750s, and by 1881 a hotel and resort with fifty rooms had grown up around them. It operated until 1920. Water from Mount Vernon Springs was bottled and sold around the South, touted for its ability to address conditions as far-ranging as "kidney and stomach troubles, teething children, nervous and rundown men and women."

Whatever the waters' curative powers, today Mount Vernon Springs is a tranquil and seemingly overlooked spot. A series of newspaper clippings under the old wooden shelter chronicles their history, mentioning that "it has always been the custom at Mount Vernon Springs for one person of a party to descend into the low area and hand up cups of water to his companions, asking which spring they wish to drink from, Health or Beauty? Young ladies always requested a mixture of both."

It's hard to know which pipe is which—the nameplates are gone, if they were ever there. Either way, you can't lose.

Get you some. The spa-gone-south is located on State Road 1134 in Chatham County.

Just Passing Through

Norlina

OK, so it's a tiny town, with a population somewhere near 1,000. But the number of people who have passed through Norlina, a trading path and transportation route for hundreds of years, can't be counted.

"For the millions of interstate travelers that visit North Carolina each year," the town's Web site notes, "Norlina is nothing more than a couple of signs along I–85." In some ways, it was a similar situation a century ago, when the place was little more than a railroad stop with a small community church and hotel famous for its "quail on toast." In 1913 community residents convinced Raleigh to grant them a town charter—even though the town's domain amounted to just one square mile.

This modest municipality, fixed just south of the border with Virginia, adopted the appropriately compact name of Norlina. The "Nor" refers to the town's status as "the first part of the North," the "lina" to its role as "the last part of Carolina."

So it's most fitting that the town "where North Carolina begins" is the place where a railroad car has come to rest, and all the more so because of what it holds today.

The Norlina Museum is housed in a dining car donated by the U.S. Army's Transportation Corps. For years it served as the town's library, but today it's home to displays on the area's history, from the railroad era and further back in time. Rarely has one rail car covered so much ground—from Native American arrowheads to colonial relics to a most-fitting modern feature: a model train that circles this museum within a train.

The museum is located in Norlina Junction Park. For touring information call (252) 456–2422 or visit www.norlina.com.

BIG HOLE'S DEEP SECRET

Ask former Pittsboro mayor Chuck Devinney what he did when he worked for AT&T, and he offers evasions straight out of an *X-Files* script. "We don't speak of it," he says. "I wiped it all out of my head. When I went out the door, I never looked back."

OK, so he doesn't want to talk about it. In fact, he's probably legally obligated not to. But if you do a little digging, you can unearth most of the dirt on what AT&T and the Defense Department were doing with an underground bunker complex in rural Chatham County.

The place has gone by various names. Some call it the Spy Hotel, but most call it Big Hole. It's a hole all right—a black hole of government secrets. But most of them have seeped out by now, so it's time to shed a little light on the place.

Chatham's underground enigma is located about 1 mile south of Fearrington Village, a few miles north of Pittsboro. It sits at the end of the appropriately named Big Hole Road, off Mount Gilead Church Road. There, Devinney and dozens of other AT&T employees holed up for much of the Cold War, soldiers in a hidden battle to safeguard the U.S. command and control system in the event of a nuclear war.

The system, called the Automatic Voice Network (AUTOVON), was started in 1964 by the Defense Communications Agency, and the Chatham facility joined the network in 1966. It was one of twenty protected AUTOVON centers that were underground, hardened facilities, engineered to withstand anything short of a direct hit by an enemy missile.

Peeking through the 10-foot-high chain-link and barbed-wire fences that circle the facility, the occasional trespasser sees a 60-car parking lot, manicured grassy knolls, a tiny guard shack, a battery of floodlight and surveillance camera posts, and, in the middle of it all, the tips of Big Hole's iceberg: a group of concrete and silver structures jutting out at odd angles. The largest is roughly two stories high, a boxy building covered with transmitters, antennae, satellite dishes, and other communications gear.

Details about the facility from former employees have surfaced in the local press, describing the high-tech fallout shelter that lies beneath. Reportedly, the entire underground portion, which descends several floors, is suspended from a superstructure ceiling to cushion bomb blasts. The bottom floor sits on a shock-absorbing cradle of gravel and coils. The walls, 18 inches thick, are sheathed in copper to deflect electromagnetic pulse.

When the facility was active, power generators were backed up with immense fuel stores, and there were bunks, medical supplies, and food sufficient for a staff of about thirty to stay underground for at least three weeks, the reports said. A decontamination chamber and filtering system would keep the air breathable in the event of nuclear war.

Fortunately for all of us, Big Hole's nuclear war capabilities were never tested. Meanwhile, AUTOVON evolved into a global communications system that carried all kinds of military messages, from the high priority to the mundane. It became, among other things, a free long-distance telephone service for military personnel. A 1987 Defense Communications Agency report said that the system was handling 1.1 million calls a day.

But don't expect anyone who worked there to brag about it. Devinney retired from Big Hole in 1996, and years later he was still sticking to the code of silence. "I still don't understand why anybody even cares about it," he says. "There's just nothing there."

Pleased to Meat You
Pittsboro

Large meat-eaters (namely the big cats) represent some of the world's most interesting—and, sadly, endangered—species. For years the Carnivore Preservation Trust (CPT), located in Pittsboro, served as an out-of-the-way breeding facility and sanctuary for lions, tigers, and a host of other rare cats. In 2005 the nonprofit opened its doors to the public, welcoming visits and financial support from the ranks of the curious.

CPT was founded in 1981 by UNC–Chapel Hill geneticist Michael Bleyman as a site for captive breeding of endangered species. After Bleyman's death in 1996, the trust took on

It pays to heed the signs at the Carnivore Preservation Trust.

an added duty as a sanctuary. Today, species on hand include ten tigers (with names as stately as Shalimar and goofy as Jellybean), five spotted leopards, and one rare snow leopard, as well as a menagerie of lesser-known animals: binturongs, caracals, kinkajous, ocelots, and servals.

Not all the animals are what you'd call fierce or meat-hungry; the Southeast Asian binturong, for instance, subsists primarily on the fruit of the strangler fig. (It does, admittedly, flash its teeth at the occasional grub, bird egg, or rodent.)

Along with the animals on display, the fifty-five-acre center grounds serve a vital and growing role as a destination for rescued animals, a place where panthers and lions too big or fierce for their quirky owners can live on without fear of being euthanized.

A recent fund-raising effort netted CPT $15,000, much of which has been used to construct a 1,500-square-foot quarantine area to house sick animals, complete with fencing capable of holding the big cats in.

Visitors must call ahead and reserve a time to visit. (Eek! Adults accompanying minors must sign a release form.) The tours, which are guided by center volunteers, at times pass within 12 feet of the big cats, albeit with steel fencing in between. It may be as close to these lords of the jungle, steppe, and savanna as you'll ever get.

To reach the Carnivore Preservation Trust, take exit 293 off I–40 onto U.S. Highway 1/Highway 64 West. Travel approximately 3 miles and exit onto Highway 64 West. Go 17 miles, crossing over Lake Jordan and the Haw River. After crossing the river, take the first left onto Foxfire Trace. Go half a mile and turn left on Dee Farrell Road. Continue to Hanks Chapel Road and turn left. CPT is located just less than half a mile on the right. To schedule a visit, call (919) 542–4684. Visit www.cptigers .org for more information.

An Everyman's Shangri-La
Prospect Hill

If you build it, they will come—especially if you build a little fantasy world that defies easy explanation.

Call him the mayor of "Shangri-La," which is what Henry Warren (1883–1977) came to name his unique creation. A retired tobacco farmer, Warren used stone, shells, concrete, and loads of ephemera to build a whimsical, miniature domain. It looks like the kind of place where you'd go to meet gnomes for tea.

It started with a waterwheel next to a goldfish pond. From there, Warren built a mill house, a house, a store, and so on. By the time he was done, there were twenty-seven structures, all woven together in a way that seems both oddly out of place and just about perfect. "As long as he had a cigarette and Coca-Cola, he'd keep building," his wife would later recall.

Shangri-La sits next to Highway 86 a few miles north of Prospect Hill and a few miles south of Hightowers, next to the community's volunteer fire department.

Henry Warren's Shangri-La is a small world for big dreamers.

OSWALD CALLING?

If you wander far enough into the hall of mirrors that is JFK assassination theorizing, you just might wind up following a trail to North Carolina. A gnawing example of the unresolved and potentially important tangents in the case (or so some researchers argue) is accused assassin Lee Harvey Oswald's so-called "Raleigh call."

Grover Proctor, who grew up in Raleigh and went on to become a university dean in Michigan, has done the most in-depth research on the matter. He wrote up his main findings back in 1980, in a two-part series for Raleigh's *Spectator* weekly, and has since posted them on the Internet with regular updates.

Here's what Proctor and other researchers have learned: Arrested within two hours after Kennedy was shot, Oswald made several phone calls from the Dallas jail in the two days before he, too, was gunned down. He called his wife, Marina Oswald, and arranged for her and his mother to visit him in jail. He called Marina's friend and benefactor, Ruth Paine, and asked her to try to contact a radical New York attorney, John Abt, while himself making fruitless attempts to reach Abt. And, late on the night of November 23, 1963—Oswald's last night alive—he evidently tried to place a call to a Raleigh resident by the name of John Hurt.

A Dallas municipal switchboard employee filled out a phone slip documenting the attempted call, which was placed by one of her colleagues. Or, rather, Oswald requested that the call be placed, but it appears that the switchboard operator only pretended to attempt the call and then told Oswald it would not go through. Whether she did this of her own volition or at the urging of Secret Service or FBI agents remains unclear.

But it does appear clear enough, based on the available records, that Oswald wanted to reach one John Hurt of Raleigh. The Dallas jail phone slip lists two numbers from the 919 area code, for two different men: John W. Hurt and John D. Hurt. Evidently, Oswald had the name in his head, or someone assisting him obtained the numbers by calling directory assistance, because they weren't in his address book.

Both John Hurts were interviewed by officials investigating the assassination, and both said they didn't know Oswald and had never spoken with him. John W., an auto mechanic, seemed a most unlikely suspect. John D., however, aroused some interest among conspiracy buffs. Although he worked as an insurance claims adjuster in the 1950s and 1960s, during World War II he had served in army counterintelligence.

Was John D. Hurt, who died in 1981, some sort of military intelligence contact for Oswald? Or perhaps an intermediary to help Oswald relay a message to his "handlers," if he had any? Or maybe it was all just some weird, scattershot historical coincidence. The possibilities, as Proctor outlines them in his report, are intriguing, if largely speculative.

"Is this the linchpin of the case?" Proctor asks. "No. But it just might shed light on some of the other things that went on."

Proctor's report, "The Raleigh Call," along with supporting documentation, is available online at www.groverproctor.us/jfk.

Polly Wants a Second Chance

Raleigh

The little stuffed bird could be mistaken for a mere footnote among the vast holdings at Raleigh's Museum of Natural Sciences, but it represents a whopper of a cautionary tale.

Prior to going extinct on us, the Carolina parakeet (*Conuropsis carolinensis*) was the only species of parrot native to the continental United States. It was widespread, ranging from haunts in the Ohio River Valley south to the Gulf Coast. It was especially fond of low, dense woods bordering creeks, rivers, and swamps. It had green wings and a similarly

The Carolina parakeet: The bad end of a good bird.

hued underbelly, with a baby-blue tinge along its back and a really dashing yellow head.

Settlers killed it for its valuable feathers, to protect their fruit crops from marauding flocks, or simply for the thrill of killing something so dumb and prodigious. As swamps were drained and woods were cleared for farmland, the bird also lost vital habitat.

Of course, the parakeet itself didn't help matters; its color scheme was trouble enough, but it also had the poignant and ultimately devastating habit of flocking around birds that had been recently killed, making it ripe for the shooting.

The parakeets were so common that likely no one imagined they would one day be goners, but, nevertheless, the last confirmed wild bird was gunned down in 1904. The last captive Carolina parakeet, a male named Incas, died at the Cincinnati Zoo in 1918, within a year of his lovely mate, Lady Jane.

Although parakeets continued to be sighted in and around southern swamps until 1930, scientists are in pretty wide agreement that the Carolina parakeet's day has come and gone, with considerable help from the hand of man.

Extinction may be forever, but you can get an idea of what you're missing by visiting the Raleigh Museum of Natural Sciences. Its bird collection is one of the best in the South (and the biggest in the state), with 20,000 specimens in storage. Most of these, of course, are not available for viewing, but two of the rarest species—the late, lamented passenger pigeon and the beautiful but doomed Carolina parakeet— are on view for guests.

The museum is located at 11 West Jones Street in Raleigh (on Bicentennial Plaza, between the capitol and legislature buildings). Admission is free, except for special exhibits. Hours are 9:00 A.M. to 5:00 P.M., Monday through Saturday, and noon to 5:00 P.M. on Sunday. Call (919) 733–7450 or visit www.naturalsciences.org.

It's Only Natural

Raleigh

There's a little-known group in the Triangle that says they've got nothing to hide. Or, if we can rephrase it, at least they don't hide anything.

"TAN is a friendly bunch of folks who like to get together about once a month and socialize," explains the group's Web site. "The only difference between us and any other group is that most activities are nude."

Oh, that *is* different. But the Triangle Area Naturists, one of at least three nude-friendly clubs in North Carolina (see the Charlotte and Outer Banks entries for the other two), feel quite free to display their differences, so to speak.

And don't get the wrong idea, the Web site advises. "There are a lot of assumptions out there about nudism and naturism among the general public, so let's dispel a few myths. Naturists are not swingers. Naturism is all about non-sexual nudity. . . . Naturists aren't all a bunch of hippie freaks. We are your neighbors, your co-workers, maybe even your accountant."

For more information and a membership application, visit www .trianglenaturists.com. (And for the record, if our accountant does our taxes in the buff, we'd just rather not know.)

Gray Matters

Raleigh

For anyone who's ever wondered what's going on inside someone's head, here's your chance to get a firsthand look.

Among the wonders at the Alice Aycock Poe Center for Health Education is a walk-in brain, more formally known as the Cranium Connection.

The Poe Center, with its interactive exhibits that make it fun to learn about bodily functions, opened in 1991 as a resource for child and family wellness education. Along with the brain, the center features TAM, the Transparent Anatomical Mannequin.

The Poe Center caters only to school groups; if you manage to pull one together, visit www.poehealth.org for more information about a visit. The center is located at 224 Sunnybrook Road, north of Poole Road, just west of U.S. Highway 440.

I Spy, You Spy

Raleigh

James Bond, don't even think about retiring.

The Cold War may be over, but the intrigue surrounding espionage is hardly on ice. North Carolina, of all places, has become a hotbed of intelligence intrigue, thanks to the annual Raleigh International Spy Conference.

Held every August since 2003 at the North Carolina Museum of History, the conference is the brainchild of publisher and spy buff Bernie Reeves. He brings together leading academics, authors, and former intelligence officials to revisit key chapters in hidden history. CIA, FBI, KGB—name your top-secret agency, and it's there.

Each conference has a central theme. Thus far, the gathering has addressed the Cold War at large, modern-day terrorism, and struggles between the United States and two of its communist enemies—China and Cuba.

Serious stuff, for sure. But it's all covered with a surprising dose of fun, as former opponents in the "great game" find the time to talk and drink together (true to the stereotype, most spies can hold their liquor). In addition to all of the chitchat about matters undercover, there are exhibits of real-life spy gear that would make Bond blush.

Surprisingly, you don't need a security clearance to be there. But you do need a ticket. To get one, and to get the goods on next year's spy gala, visit www.raleighspyconference.com.

The Whimsical Mansion

Reidsville

When Jeff and Betsy Penn decided to build their dream house, they dreamt a little harder than most of us do. They broke ground on it in 1923, and by the time they were done two years later, they had a twenty-seven-room mansion just waiting to be filled with every curio under the sun.

The twenty-two-acre Chinqua-Penn Plantation, as they called it, didn't have to wait long. (The name was a play on the couple's surname and the chinquapin tree, a diminutive chestnut that was abundant around the property at the time.) The Penns were wealthy collectors and world travelers with delightfully eccentric tastes.

Stepping inside their luxurious lair, visitors encountered room after room of some of the finest—and strangest—items that could be found in any corner of the world: fantastic vintage furniture; an organ with 1,000 pipes that played itself; and remarkable works of art, including an ornate relief sculpture of the life of Buddha. The Chinese room, the Italian room, and the astoundingly lush velvet room, where the walls were covered in silk velvet, were just a few of the mansion's allures. And aside from all the treasure-filled rooms, the plantation boasted twenty-two acres of grand gardens and fountains.

In the late 1960s, after both of the Penns had died, their family donated the land to the state of North Carolina, which ran Chinqua-Penn as a museum for twenty or so years. From the 1990s until recent times, the estate has been managed first by a private foundation and then by North Carolina State University.

Lately, the Penns' wonder world has lain dormant, but not for long: In July 2006 the state sold Chinqua-Penn to Mocksville tobacco company owner Calvin Phelps. He paid just over $4 million for the joint—a pretty good bargain, many said at the time. Phelps and his wife say that they plan to allow for at least occasional public access to the place—perhaps holiday tours—though they haven't worked out the specifics.

"We know it has been part of the community and it should remain part of the community," Phelps said when he bought it. And he and his wife surely do know: They paid their first visit to the odd splendor of Chinqua-Penn decades ago, during what happened to be their first date.

For now, the best way to see the place is online, where N.C. State hosts a thorough multimedia tour. Take it at www.chinquapenn.com.

To the Moon
Rhodhiss

Rhodhiss (population 897) may be a small town, but it's got an "out of this world" claim to fame.

'Twas a proud day for most Americans and perhaps most earthlings when, on July 20, 1969, astronaut Neil Armstrong became the first

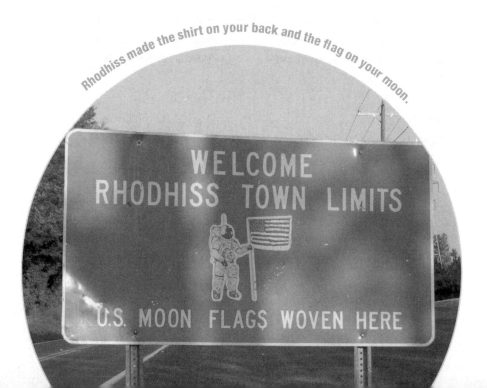

Rhodhiss made the shirt on your back and the flag on your moon.

human to set foot on the moon. One of the first acts of Armstrong's crew was to plant the Stars and Stripes in the rocky surface.

The United States didn't claim the moon as U.S. territory, but over the years American astronauts left no fewer than six U.S. flags—one for each lunar mission—there in the manner that explorers do when they claim new ground. (Talk about your amusement parks: Six Flags over the Moon, anyone?)

You won't see much mention of it in the history books, but the durable nylon used to make those flags was manufactured in Rhodhiss, at a now-defunct mill next to the dam in the center of town.

Rhodhiss is located about 8 miles northwest of Hickory. Coming into town from either the north or the south, you'll pass astronaut-bearing signs noting one of North Carolina's little-known contributions to space exploration. It's a rare town that can boast: "U.S. Moon Flags Woven Here."

Tickets to Ride
Shelby

Trains, it seems, come in two sizes: the big 'uns that ride the rails and helped industrialize America, and the miniature variety beloved by model train enthusiasts.

Well, in fact, there's a third size, at least in Shelby. In 1952 the local chapter of the Rotary Club bought a small but rideable rig from the Miniature Train Company and installed it in Shelby City Park. Over the decades it fell into disrepair and disuse, but in 2002 locals rallied to get the wheels turning again, restoring it and building a tunnel and small-scale depot. Fortunately, inflation hasn't kept up with all the improvements; today, you can ride the train for the decidedly old-fashioned price of 50 cents.

The train has an engine and three coach cars. It's a quick ride around the racetrack-shaped route, but a mighty fun one, especially for kids (and the young at heart).

But don't stop there. After a few rounds on the rails, you can spin around another of the park's unusual amusements: a fully functioning, lovingly restored 1919 carousel. The ride was installed in 1952 as well and has a similar history of neglect and renewal. Today, almost 50,000 people take a turn on it each year.

The mini-train is open at Shelby City Park (851 West Sumpter Street) from March to November, with some special holiday hours in the winter. The carousel is open year-round. For directions and details about hours, call (704) 484–6476 or visit www.cityofshelby.com.

The Devil's Tramping Ground

Siler City

It gets hot in parts of Chatham County, but surely not as hot as hell. So Ol' Scratch—aka Beelzebub, the Lord of Darkness, the Devil—can't be blamed for taking a little time out from Hades to stroll in the relatively cool Carolina nights.

Turns out that this most devilish of dudes has his very own spot here, or so it would appear. As far back as anyone can remember, there has existed a circle in a clearing in the woods, 40 feet in diameter, where nothing is said to grow. The name imparted on the place— Devil's Tramping Ground—makes it pretty clear who's been treading that circle for lo these many years.

He comes at night, people say, and walks in circles, all the while plotting mayhem, tragedy, temptation, and the like. The Devil's work is dirty business, of course, and his circle of sin is a testament to the many hours he must spend concocting plans to bring doom to us all, so the story goes.

Or is it just that enough visitors show up and tramp on the circle that no vegetation grows on it? Suggest that to anyone who believes the stories, and they'll tell you that's blasphemy.

We found the place a diabolical letdown—this is one circle that seems anything but unbroken. For starters, patches of grass have obscured and invaded the shape. So has a smattering of broken glass and other litter. True, there was a *Blair Witch Project*–style configuration of twigs on the ground, but it just wasn't enough.

Chigger bites, bewilderment, and much, much more: the Devil's Tramping Ground.

In frustration, we called the Devil out: "Satan, can you spiff the joint up a little bit? This is *so* not scary."

Maybe, we thought, we've just found the wrong spot. So we plunged farther into the woods, searching in vain for more devilish signs. We found nothing but a maze of forking trails, thick brush, and the occasional set of deer bones.

But, oh, that cursed critter may have been there after all, and evidently he didn't care for our disdain. Later in the day, we found ourselves covered in chigger bites. Were those little red mites who gave us so many oozing sores the Devil's minions? Sure felt like it.

Should any of you saints or sinners care to walk a circle in the Dark One's shoes, the Devil's Tramping Ground is located on State Road 1100, about 10 miles south of Siler City and 1 mile north of Highway 902, at Harper's Crossroads. A small dirt parking spot marks the entry. Do *not* go into the woods.

The First Golden State
Stanfield

Oh, sure, Californians will tell you that their state is where the United States struck gold, but sorry, folks—Tar Heels had you beat by a good fifty years.

John Reed was a retired Hessian soldier who left the British army and settled in Cabarras County. One Sunday in 1799, his son, Conrad, discovered a seventeen-pound, shiny rock in a creek on the family's farm. They thought it a good find, though not in the way you might expect: They used it as a doorstop for three years.

In 1802 they sold the rock to a Fayetteville jeweler for a measly $3.50. They should have asked for closer to $3,500—the actual value of the doorstop, which in fact was a sizable gold nugget.

So it went with the first documented gold find in the United States. The Reeds got smart at that point and started the country's first gold-mining operation. The first year it operated, a slave named Peter turned up an even bigger, twenty-eight-pound nugget. By 1824 the Reed mine had yielded an estimated $100,000 in gold—quite a sizable sum in that day—simply from sifting creek gravel. A few years later, the Reeds went undergound, mining for gold veins in white quartz rock.

Meanwhile, a lower Piedmont gold craze came and went; at its peak in 1830, the state was home to fifty-six gold mines. In 1848 gold discoveries in California sent would-be miners west. Still, the Reed mine remained in operation until 1912.

Today, this nugget of North Carolina history is preserved by the state's Office of Archives and History, which maintains the Reed Gold Mine State Historic Site in Stanfield. It's open most days, depending on the season, and admission is free (though panning for gold flakes requires a nominal fee). Visitors can tour restored mine shafts and get an up-close look at historical mining equipment, including an ore-crushing stamp mill. Talk about your golden opportunities . . .

Stanfield is located about 20 miles northeast of Charlotte. For directions, hours, and other details, call (704) 721–4653 or visit www.ah.dcr .state.nc.us/sections/hs/reed/reed.htm.

High Chair

Thomasville

If, heaven help us, Godzilla were ever to come shambling into downtown Thomasville, residents might ease his rampage a bit by inviting him to sit down. Few towns have chairs big enough to accommodate such giant guests. This tidy Piedmont city is one.

Measuring 18 feet tall (ignoring its slab limestone base), the replica Duncan Phyfe chair towers above the town center but garners hardly a turned head in Thomasville, which for decades has been known for its furniture industry, especially its fine chairs.

The chair is actually the second one at this location; the first was built in 1922 to make good on a boast from Charles Sturkey, managing editor of the weekly *Chair Town News*. Sturkey said the town would build the world's biggest chair, and when a retraction seemed out of the question,

Take a load off, Goliath.

the Thomasville Chair Company (today Thomasville Furniture Industries) took up the challenge and built a solid-pine specimen that was 13.5 feet tall and upholstered (or, uphol*steer*ed is more like it) from the hide of one especially unlucky Swiss steer.

In time the chair decayed, but the pride of Thomasvillians didn't, so in 1948 the Chamber of Commerce set about getting one built that would last.

Dedicated in 1951, version two is constructed of cement and steel, with brass rods providing the elegant curves of the chair's back. No less than President Lyndon Johnson once sat in it, as well as several Misses America. Don't try it yourself without permission from the City Fathers (and Mothers).

The chair to end all chairs is located at the corner of Randolph and Main Streets in downtown Thomasville.

Gracias, Lazaro
Waxhaw

It's a rare Mexican president who has a museum dedicated to him in the United States. And as far as we know, only one has earned that honor in the Tar Heel State.

Gen. Lazaro Cárdenas (1895–1970) served as Mexico's president from 1934 to 1940, winning respect as one of that country's first modern reformers. One of his first acts in office was to slash his salary in half. He also took the unprecedented step of firing and deporting corrupt higher-ups in his government and decreed an end to capital punishment. What's more, he advanced a form of Mexican nationalism that paid heed to *all* of the country's residents, indigenous and Spanish descendants alike.

It was that latter quality that earned Cárdenas some lifelong friends in the United States. Among the best of them was Cameron Townsend (1896–1982), who made it his life's work to promote the study and documentation of all the world's languages—especially those that were spoken by groups so small or remote that their linguistic traditions stood a chance of disappearing. A corollary goal was to translate the Bible into as many tongues as possible.

In the mid-1930s Townsend founded the Summer Institute of Linguistics and Wycliffe Bible Translators, and his mission took him to indigenous villages in Mexico where nary a person spoke Spanish. Hearing of Townsend's work, Cárdenas was both intrigued and supportive. The two men forged an informal partnership to promote the study and understanding of Mexican Indian languages.

Townsend never forgot Cárdenas's assistance, and the translator later published one of the first biographies of the Mexican leader. Cárdenas died in 1970. Seven years later, Townsend opened the Mexico-Cárdenas Museum to make sure that the two men's collaboration would have its rightful place in history. At the museum you can view displays detailing Mexican history and Cárdenas's crucial role in modernizing the country, rare pieces of Mexican folk art, jewelry and traditional attire, a sizable bust of Cárdenas, and a 1938 Chevrolet sedan that the Mexican president donated to help Townsend's team of translators record native languages and deliver health services in remote regions.

The free museum, which is supported by donations, is open Monday through Saturday from 9:00 A.M. to noon and from 1:00 to 3:30 P.M. It's located at 6400 Davis Road in Waxhaw. For directions and other details, call (704) 843–6066 or visit www.jaars.org/museums.shtml.

Alphabet Soup

Waxhaw

A-B-C is not necessarily as easy as 1-2-3. It's a big old world out there, and most of us have trouble enough mastering our own language, much less trying to communicate with people in every corner of the globe. But that's what Cameron Townsend set out to do (see the previous entry), in the service of both preserving every ethnic group's way of speaking and making sure said groups could read the Bible.

Today, his work is carried on by JAARS Inc., which runs the Museum of the Alphabet. A kind of world headquarters of the written word, the museum presents the trials and tribulations of alphabet-makers through time.

It's an appropriately enormous facility, occupying 4,900 square feet. After passing through an introductory room, visitors take a walking tour of the history of alphabets as they developed in places near and far. While some displays record the achievements of broad groups of people, others focus on key individuals like North Carolina's own Sequoia, the Cherokee Indian who almost single-handedly crafted his people's first full alphabet.

A scrap metal sculpture by Alan Baughman is featured in the introductory room. Fittingly, it depicts the Tower of Babel, where, the Bible says, man overreached himself by trying to build a structure that would climb to heaven. God's punishment, the story goes, was to confound Babel's workers by imbuing them with different languages; since they couldn't understand one another, they quit working and spread out to populate the rest of the earth.

So maybe it's only fitting that at the Museum of the Alphabet, some of the Bible's biggest modern-day fans are determined to reconnect the world's disparate languages and the alphabets they're made of.

The museum's hours, location, and contact information are the same as the Mexico-Cárdenas Museum, which is listed in the previous entry.

What Two Can Do

White Plains

Chang and Eng Bunker were closer than most brothers. Much closer.

Conjoined twins from Siam (Thailand) who were born in 1811, Chang and Eng were connected at the chest by a 6-inch-wide band of flesh. They spent their entire lives walking, eating, and sleeping in tandem, "living together" in a way that would bring new meaning to the notion. Today, when you hear the term "Siamese twins," it's because the brothers' remarkable lives gave rise to the phrase.

In 1829 a Scottish trader named Robert Hunter arranged to transport the boys, whom he had met when they were working as street peddlers in Bangkok, to the United States. Instant globe-trotters, Chang and Eng appeared as "The Double Boys" in the Barnum circus, marveling crowds from New York to London to the American heartland.

Chang and Eng Bunker coined the term "Siamese twins." The brothers are shown with two of their several sons.

Carving out some fame and a small fortune by putting themselves on display, the twins left Barnum at age twenty-one to run their own tours. But they soon tired of the rigors of being on display and decided to seek out a quieter life.

And so, in 1839, the brothers moved to Mount Airy, where they ran a store for a short time and bought a farm. Then they found love: After a strained but ultimately fruitful courtship with two sisters on a neighboring farm, Chang and Eng married Adelaide and Sarah, respectively. And lest anyone think that being stuck together kept the brothers from enjoying the full fruits of married life, consider only that Chang fathered ten children and Eng fathered twelve.

But they did much more than make babies: They ran their farm and worked as woodcutters. They played chess and poker and indulged their shared interests in fine clothing and good cigars. When times got tight after the Civil War, they even took their show out on the road a few more times, again touring Europe.

Resilient and innovative to the end, the twins passed away in 1874 at age sixty-two. Chang, who had suffered a stroke some months before, went first, and Eng followed two hours later.

The "original Siamese twins" left a family legacy that ranks among the most unique in North Carolina's history (and the entire country's, for that matter). Today, their descendants number close to 1,500. Interestingly, that number includes eleven sets of twins, according to an article on the Bunker family's annual reunion in the June 2006 *National Geographic* magazine.

To see where these uncommon twins came to rest, visit their gravesite at the Old White Plains Baptist Church on old U.S. Highway 601, 2 miles west of Mount Airy.

Where Tom Dooley Hung His Head

Wilkesboro

North Carolina history is full of villains, louts, no-goods, murderers, cheats, and layabouts. Who knows? Maybe it's the water, or something drifting along in our balmy air.

One of the state's most famous bad men was Tom Dula, a Wilkes County native whose alleged murder of Laura Foster, in 1866, became the story behind one of the most popular songs in the folk repertoire. When the Kingston Trio went platinum in 1958 with the refrain "Hang down your head, Tom Dooley . . . hang down your head and cry," they were talking about this guy.

Dula, a Civil War veteran, notable musician, and all-around handsome, charming fellow, returned from military service and settled down here. Or did he? Dula, happily ensconced in one relationship, purportedly courted another young woman named Laura Foster, and, just before eloping with her, killed her in a poetic, made-for-song fashion—stabbing her through the heart and burying her in a shallow grave.

Foster's body was eventually stumbled upon, and a manhunt began. Days later, Dula was discovered in eastern Tennessee, apparently without a watertight alibi. He was hauled back and kept here, in the Old Wilkes Jail, until his lawyer, former governor Zebulon Vance, managed to get a change of venue. Despite Vance's aid, Dula ended up going to the gallows, claiming his innocence to the end.

The Old Wilkes Jail was nearly new when Dula paced his cell here; the brick building was constructed in 1859 and opened for service the next year. During the Civil War it served as a depot for Confederate provisions and a holding place for Union prisoners.

Dula wasn't the only notable incarcerated at the jail; the famous escape artist Otto Wood, who later went on the lam from ten jails before being shot dead by police in Salisbury, North Carolina, in 1930, was held here when he was just fifteen for stealing a bicycle.

The restored jail has all of its solid doors and iron bars lovingly restored, including a front door studded with so many nails that a would-be escapee could not, try as he might, saw his way out. Today, it's operated by the nonprofit Old Wilkes Inc. and is open, free of charge, Monday through Friday and on weekends by appointment. It is located at 203 North Bridge Street in Wilkesboro. Call (336) 667–3712 or visit www.wilkesboro.com/oldwilkesinc for information.

Jesse Helms Forever

Wingate

The United States is a country full of former senators who were both powerful and on the margins, ideologically speaking. Few of them get a permanent memorial. Jesse Helms happens to be one who did.

Funded with money from tobacco companies, Kuwaiti oil barons, and plenty of regular Americans, the Jesse Helms Center stands as a truly unique landmark of statesmanship that was conducted from the fringe. During his five terms in Congress, Helms managed to irritate—but sometimes still deal with—a startling number of players in national and international politics. Along the way he left a legacy that might surprise many who observed his divisive career, were they to visit the center built in his name.

The center, which is probably best described as a museum in the making, features displays on the senator's life and career, as he rose from North Carolina's preeminent right-wing crusader to the nation's preeminent right-wing crusader. The displays also include a tribute to North Carolina's leading entrepreneurs, and even a mock-up of the United Nations, which Helms almost always held in contempt.

The Jesse Helms Center (3910 Highway 74E in Wingate) is open from 9:00 A.M. to 5:00 P.M., Monday through Friday. The Web site address is www.jessehelmscenter.org.

Check Your Oil?

Winston–Salem

In the 1930s, seeking to lure motorists to its Shell Oil stations, Winston-Salem–based Quality Oil built eight stations in the shape of—what else?—giant shells. Fashioned from cement stucco laid over a wire and green wood framework, the stations were painted the eye-searing yellow trademarked by Royal Dutch-Shell. The pint-size stations were a triumph of functional advertising, with a great helping of Art Deco styling thrown in. Moreover, they made a guy feel good about gassing up.

Today, just one of them is left. In time the lone mollusk's condition was allowed to slide, and, through the 1970s and 1980s, it became something of a commercial urchin, seeing use as a lawn mower repair shop.

In the late 1990s the nonprofit Preservation North Carolina saw what a pearl the place could be and undertook the job of restoring it, at a cost of $50,000, with assistance from Quality Oil, the Shell Oil Company, and the John Wesley and Anna Hodgin Hanes Foundation, as well as individual donors. Workers stripped away layers of paint to reveal the scallop's original hue and repaired the station door, as well as an attached car wash that was feeling its years. Quality Oil even donated the pair of old-school gas pumps out front to complete the air of renewal.

Today, Preservation North Carolina (www.presnc.org) uses the station as an auxiliary office and information center. To reach the giant shell, take the Clemmonsville Road exit off I–40. Turn left onto East Sprague Street and continue to the intersection with Peachtree Street.

A vintage Shell station that's ribbed for your pleasure.

SAY WHAT?

Before you set out across North Carolina to see some curiosities, you may want to avoid embarrassment by learning (at the very least) how to say the names of the counties you'll pass through.

We can't help you with all the names of the Tar Heel State's towns and cities (for instance, whether to say Manteo as Man-TAY-o or MAN-eo); it's too big a job, and we're hardly experts. But if you visit "Talk Like a Tar Heel" (www.lib.unc.edu/ncc/ref/resources/tlth .html), you'll get an idea of how to say the state's one hundred counties.

There, North Carolina authors Bland Simpson and Michael McPhee try their darnedest to represent the county names the way locals say them. You'll find out that it's TEER-ull, not TY-rell, and other surprises.

Once you master the counties, the Web site also gives a selection of some of the state's most mispronounced locales. Next time you visit Conetoe, you won't be laughed out of town by pronouncing it like the combination of a geometric figure and a lower-body appendage. It's kuh-NEE-tuh, after all.

PUT 'EM UP!

Along with fiddling, boasting, singing, card-playing, tippling, pipe-packing, and general hell-raising, men in early North Carolina loved to fight. Fighting was a form of recreation, a way of settling scores, and a way of maiming people you didn't like. Friends fought. Enemies fought. Brothers fought. Fathers and sons fought.

People called the style of fighting "rough-and-tumble" or "gouging," and the emphasis was on disfigurement, up to and including ripping opponents' noses off and scooping their eyeballs out with a thumb or forefinger. It comes as no surprise that the contests generally were preceded with liberal consumption of spirits, bragging, and a series of taunts and putdowns. ("You couldn't write your way out of a hempen sack," or "That's so incurious it's curious.")

The no-holds-barred style of fighting was noticed by the authorities as early as 1746, when North Carolina's colonial governor

From Harden E. Taliaferro's *Fisher's River* (North Carolina) *Scenes and Characters . . .* (1859)

begged legislators to prohibit "the barbarous and inhuman manner of boxing which so much prevails among the lower sort of people." The state's colonial assembly responded in kind by making it a felony "to cut out the Tongue or pull out the eyes of the King's Liege People." A half decade later the violence had not abated, and North Carolina's lawmakers added slitting, biting, and removal of noses by force to the list of punishable offenses. Nevertheless, gouging refused to go away and, instead, just moved west with the frontier.

An English traveler afoot in Georgia described this match between a native of that state and a visiting Tar Heel:

> We found the combatants . . . fast clinched by the hair, and their thumbs endeavoring to force a passage into each other's eyes; while several of the bystanders were betting upon the first eye to be turned out of its socket. For some time the combatants avoided the thumb stroke with dexterity. At length they fell to the ground, and in an instant the uppermost sprung up with his antagonist's eye in his hand! The savage crowd applauded, while, sick with horror, we galloped away from the infernal scene. The name of the sufferer was John Butler, a Carolinian, who, it seems, had been dared to the combat by a Georgian; and the first eye was for the honor of the state to which they respectively belonged.

Thank heavens gouging is mostly a thing of our state's uncouth past. Still, most of us are unwittingly connected to that sport—every time we use the expression "saving face," in fact.

THE COASTAL PLAIN

VIRGINIA

Murfreesboro
Weldon

Merry
Hill

Rocky Mount

Bailey

Lucama

Angier

Smithfield

Grifton

Bunnlevel

Kinston

Pinehurst
Aberdeen

Southern Pines

Spivey's
Corner

Fayetteville

Red Springs

Laurinburg

SOUTH
CAROLINA

Whiteville

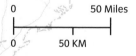

0   50 Miles

0   50 KM

THE COASTAL PLAIN

Don't let the word *plain* in *Coastal Plain* fool you—this place is anything but ordinary. Take, for example, Aberdeen, a landlocked town that nevertheless sees fit to hold a festival each year giving honor and praise to the stinky, ocean-going sardine. Or how about a collection of bells so big that it takes a village to ring them?

Here, in the big crescent of land east of Raleigh but west of the "Sound Country," you'll stumble on a museum dedicated to the tools doctors used to always have on hand, including bowls for catching blood and tonics to expel worms. If you leave that place a little woozy, head to Grifton and settle your stomach with a little fried shad. Feeling stuffed? Head to Southern Pines and take in the Taxidermy Hall of Fame.

As a place with long ties to the military, it shouldn't surprise you to find some big bases around here, including the Army's Fort Bragg, as well as Seymour Johnson and Pope Air Force bases. Jets, tanks, and rockets, fine: But how about some odder military relics, like a stuffed bear that once parachuted with troops into battle, or a nuclear bomb from the throes of the Cold War: live, mostly forgotten, and buried deep inside a swamp?

If your tastes are of a more peaceful tack, there are other things to see in this land of sand and pines: A college with a course of study in bagpipes; an Indian nation that's lost its leader; and a sky full of giant, whimsical whirligigs, stirring at the gentlest of breezes.

Your mission, should you choose to accept it, is get out and see these places. And, as always, we're here to help.

The Tin Man
Aberdeen

The sardine is sort of the Rodney Dangerfield of the seafood world—it "can't get no respect."

Or so Randall Moss discovered many years ago, when his coworkers ran him out of the company break room for eating the pungent fish one too many times.

Moss did as any sardine lover would and kept eating them. Only now he took his lunch out to a picnic table along the shore of Aberdeen Lake, where he could eat in peace.

As proof that adversity can breed triumph, Moss combined his beloved fish with that inspired lakeside setting and created a successful festival from them. The International Sardine Festival began in 1993 with Moss and four attendees. Today, it's grown into an event that attracts hundreds.

Sardines are caught along the West Coast, a world away from Aberdeen and North Carolina's landlocked Sandhills region. But that incongruity doesn't bother festivalgoers, and it clearly doesn't bother Moss. The event has even attracted a generous corporate sponsor in the Port Clyde Sardine company.

Everything is free at the International Sardine Festival, including sardines prepared three ways, fish steaks packed in oil, soda crackers, Moon Pies, and RC Cola to wash it all down with. Donations are encouraged, with proceeds going to the Aberdeen Parks and Recreation Department.

You may never learn to love the sardine—a humble fish with a proud odor—but you've got to hand it to Randall Moss, a gustatory visionary if ever there was one.

The International Sardine Festival takes place in early October. Call Randall Moss at (910) 944-1839 for more information. Aberdeen is located off U.S. Highway 1 and Highway 5, just south of Southern Pines.

The Bells Toll for Thee

Angier

The late Robert and Addie Coats found the peal of bells most appealing. Over time they collected more than twenty bells—brass, bronze, and iron ones of various sizes. Wouldn't it sound great, they thought, to hear them all ringing together?

The bevy of bells at the Coats Country Museum just begs to be rung.

And so was born a most unique belfry, of sorts. With help from neighbors and friends, the Coatses constructed a sizable metal frame for the bells, which are arranged on four tiers. Pulling a set of strategically placed ropes, you can really ring some bells.

In 1970 the couple built the Coats Country Museum on their rural family homestead. The museum holds a host of old-timey relics of country life, from farm implements to very vintage clothing to collections of antique dolls, fans, furniture, and the like—but the real highlight is the bell collection outside.

The Coatses ultimately donated the museum—bells and all—to the Pleasant Grove Township, members of which still come together to ring those bells every Independence Day. It's a cacophony that breeds community, so to speak.

The Coatses would stage ceremonial ringings of the bells on a set schedule: at 9:00 A.M. on Sunday (a chimey reminder to get to church?), at 5:00 P.M. on Easter Sunday, at noon on the Fourth of July, and at sunset on New Year's Eve. On more somber occasions the bells would occasionally toll in honor of community members who had died.

The museum is located at 3317 Old Fairground Road (State Road 1309) in Angier, 3 miles west of the intersection of Highways 50 and 210. Admission is free, but the museum is open by appointment only. To arrange a visit, call Myrline Watson at (919) 934–4763.

Gourdness Gracious!
Angier

North Carolina has never had a greater authority on gourds, or at least their artistic potential, than the late Marvin Johnson.

Johnson and his wife, Mary, started their Gourd Museum in 1965, basically because Mary was tripping over them. Her husband's love of the bulbous vegetables once led him to grow ten acres of them not far from their house, and, over the years, he had developed the habit of collecting painted gourds whenever and wherever he saw them. Too many of them, it turns out, even for a loving and supportive wife like Mary.

Like Hollywood starlets, Marvin Johnson's gourds are beautiful but hollow inside.

Rather than let a gourd thing slip away, Johnson opened a museum in a small outbuilding on his property. He filled it with handpainted gourds fashioned to look like any number of animals: snakes, penguins, frogs, sharks, owls, cats, an elephant, a killer whale. He filled it with seasonal gourds, such as the one painted to look like Santa and another that favors Rudolph the Red-Nosed Reindeer. Johnson also got his hands on a 3-foot-tall female fashioned from gourds and bearing the words "Gaudy Gourd Girl in All Gourd Garb." Her shirt and stole are made from loofah, a springy material that grows inside certain gourds. The fun doesn't stop there: There are gourds painted to look like the farm couple depicted in *American Gothic,* a gourd Popeye ("I am what I am"), a gourd xylophone, and, on a handful of timeworn gourd seeds, a representation of the Last Supper of Christ.

Johnson was an understated man who seemed delighted by the world's interest in his gourds, and he never charged admission to see them. "I've made lots of friends through gourds," he once said.

Marvin died in 2002. By then, care for the collection had passed down to his nephew, Mark Johnson. Mark in turn gave the gourds to the town of Angier, which now displays them in the town hall.

For more information, call the town at (919) 639–2071. By the way, Angier bills itself as "the town of crepe myrtles," but we're no fools. Gourds rule here.

Scars and All

Bailey

Living as we do in the world of modern medicine, it's easy to forget that doctors didn't always work in sterile, orderly environments. Used to be, the doc would often tend to what ailed you in less than ideal circumstances—and with fairly blunt instruments, at that. The proper tools (when they were available at all) weren't always clean, and sometimes guesswork was as good as the still-developing science.

But doctors working in the sticks still gave it a good go, and at the Country Doctor Museum—"the oldest museum in the United States dedicated to the history of America's rural health care"—they get their due. Founded in 1967 and run by East Carolina University since 2003, the museum is home to artifacts that are testament both to how far medical treatment has come and to the lengths it had to travel to get to its current state.

This is not exactly a little shop of horrors, but some of the relics fall on the unsettling, if still educational, side. There are rudimentary dental tools, "bleeding bowls," and a "scarificator" (don't ask, unless you want to know what bleeding bowls are for).

Other museum highlights—such as the lovely, multicolored glass "show globes" that used to adorn pharmacies—give off a healthy glow.

To check out how people used to get their checkups, you don't need an appointment—but you do need to show up when the museum is open. Hours are 10:00 A.M. to 4:00 P.M., Tuesday through Saturday. Admission is $5.00 for adults, $4.00 for seniors, and $3.00 for students. For directions, call (252) 235–4165 or visit www.countrydoctormuseum .org.

Home of the Hattadare

Bunnlevel

James N. Lowery (1912–1990) founded a nation, or at least he tried to. When the government didn't see it his way, he set about building his nation anyway.

It all began with a vision in the late 1960s, as Lowery would later explain. On three subsequent nights, he said, an apparition of Henry Berry Lowery, a Lumbee Indian outlaw hero from the Civil War era, came to him through his television, which happened to be turned off at the time. The visitor revealed to him the history of a lost Native American tribe—born of North Carolina natives and the first wave of English settlers—which James Lowery was destined to lead.

Reservation needed: The Hattadare nation lives on along a Harnett County byway.

Lowery took the name Dr. Chief Little Beaver and sought federal recognition for the tribe, which he dubbed Hattadare. The "Hatta" was a nod to the Hatteras Indians; the "dare" was derived from Virginia Dare, of lost colony fame. Over time he would sign up close to 1,000 members, but he never succeeded in getting Washington to recognize the Hattadare.

No matter, though. Lowery set about establishing a place in this world for his tribe, building what folk art scholars call a "personal history environment." He called it "The North Carolina Indian Adventure." By any name, the half-acre attraction is a poignant mix of outdoor history museum and yard-art gallery.

Today, much of the adventure remains, thanks to Lowery's family, which keeps the grounds up. You can see it pretty much how he left it: Using concrete and spackle, he constructed statues of key figures in the Hattadare Nation's history. Lowery explained how he built the place in a 1986 interview with the Raleigh *News and Observer*, which likened Lowery's park, appropriately enough, to "an orphanage for life-size cowboy and Indian toys."

"It's not made from a mold; it's all made from history and legend," he said. "I've never been to a sculpture class. But I say 'Inch by inch, anything's a cinch.' And that's how I built it."

He added, "You see, the Indian in eastern North Carolina has been lost as to his identity for 400 years. This gives them an identity. This tells 'em who they are."

Today the grounds contain most of the original statues, covered by roof sheds, and an impressive statue of Lowery himself (it was the last one he built before his death). Then there are the concrete bears, cacti, and tepees; the giant arrowhead made of concrete and rock; and the waist-high, gold-painted model of the chief's unrealized dream—a thirteen-story, pyramid-like theater that would have been used to tell Hattadare history on a grand scale.

Though what remains is a reduced version of Lowery's vision, the place still offers a remarkable trip into the world as he saw it. His son, Dennis Lowery, who still lives on the grounds, showed us around. "My daddy could do anything he wanted to do," he said.

The headquarters of the Hattadare Indian Nation is right next to Highway 401, 12 miles north of Fayetteville. If you keep an eye out for the relics mentioned above, you can't miss it.

Are You Ready for the Great Atomic Power?

Faro

In military parlance, when a nuclear weapon goes missing it's called a "broken arrow." It may sound like the stuff of Tom Clancy novels, but it actually happened—a few times too many—during the Cold War, when the United States "lost" at least eleven nukes. One of them is buried in rural North Carolina, a mere 45 miles from Raleigh.

Don't panic: The bomb has sat peacefully in a boggy grave for more than four decades, and it's all but impossible that it could explode, say nuclear weapons experts who have studied the case. Just to be on the safe side, the North Carolina Division of Radiation Protection conducts annual tests to make sure that no radioactive material has leaked from it.

So how did it get there? Shortly after midnight on January 24, 1961, an eight-man crew steered a B-52 through a winter storm on their way back home to Seymour Johnson Air Force Base in Goldsboro. The plane's bomb bay held two 2.5-megaton nuclear bombs, each roughly the size of a Volkswagen bug.

A sudden mechanical failure caused thousands of gallons of fuel to spew out of the plane, generating a fire that disabled a wing. The crew bailed out near the tiny town of Faro, roughly 10 miles from the base.

Most of the crew, and one of the two bombs, descended to the ground with parachutes. Five of the airmen survived, and the bomb that drifted down was retrieved the next day by an Air Force recovery crew, who found it partially submerged in a soggy field.

The other bomb's parachute, however, failed to deploy, and so the weapon fell like the five-ton hunk of metal, wiring, and uranium that it was. When it encountered the ground, it kept on going. Nobody knows for sure how deep it went.

A few parts did turn up: At depths of between 10 and 20 feet, excavators retrieved the bomb's tail, undeployed parachute, and pieces of its firing mechanism. But the bulk of the broken arrow had burrowed too deep to be reached. Military engineers estimated that it was buried 180 feet below the surface, and at 40 feet, with their biggest water pumps failing to stem the tide of groundwater seeping into the hole, they gave up. Subsequently, the Air Force refilled the impact site and purchased an easement that to this day prohibits any digging below 5 feet.

In 2000 a team of students at the UNC–Chapel Hill School of Journalism and Mass Communication compiled an in-depth report on the loose nuke (available online at www.ibiblio.org/bomb.html). Nuclear warfare expert Chuck Hansen, interviewed by the students, summarized the seriousness of the 1961 mishap in stark terms. "I do not now know of any other weapon accident that came this close to a full-scale nuclear detonation," he said.

If you want to get close to the bomb, travel 1.5 miles south of Faro on Big Daddy's Road. There are no markers or signs, and the bomb site is grown over and nondescript, so you'll have to ask a local to pinpoint it.

Barney the War Bear

Fayetteville

War museums face a lot of hard choices, always grappling with the question of how best to depict a history rife with hard times. The occasional one casts caution to the wind and lets it all hang out, and the JFK Special Warfare Museum at Fort Bragg—where you can meet Barney the bear—is one of them.

Barney was the mascot of the Fifth Special Forces Group–Airborne's Company Alpha, stationed in South Vietnam. The Malayan Sun bear, the story goes, was a young, orphaned cub when the soldiers picked him up.

The company of Green Berets built a special bond with the bear they named Barney. In fact, he would even "be put in a knapsack when the company parachuted into missions," according to what might be the authoritative write-up on the bear, prepared by the curiosityphiles at Roadside America (read it at www.roadsideamerica.com/pet/barney .html).

"Sgt. Jerald Hilleson was especially fond of Barney," Roadside reports. "When the sergeant's tour of duty ended, he decided to take the bear with him. He got Barney drunk, stuffed him into his duffel bag, and wedged him into the overhead bin of his 727 back to the states. Unfortunately, Barney woke up halfway over the Pacific, a very pissed-off bear. By the time Barney was through, Sgt. Hilleson was out several thousand dollars in damages, and nearly out of the Army."

Barney spent a restful two years in retirement at Fort Bragg before dying of pneumonia in 1972. He was the kind of war pet who might have garnered a stately gravestone or monument, but instead he's memorialized in the flesh: Barney's body was stuffed, and it has long resided—in a standing pose—in a Plexiglas case at the JFK Special Warfare Museum.

To this day the guy looks friendly, especially for a bear. Sure, he seems a little bit out of place in a museum dedicated to recording the exploits of commandos, but he's hardly the only unusual historical relic in the place. The museum is home to a rich and often unconventional assortment of military memorabilia.

There's a diorama of a North Vietnamese prisoner of war camp raided by special operations troops; another re-creates a life-size POW cell in Vietnam. The museum also boasts a wooden billboard of leftist firebrand Maurice Bishop taken during the U.S. invasion of Grenada in 1983, as well as more right-leaning relics, such as photos of Green Berets posing with Hollywood super-soldier John Wayne, who filmed much of his 1968 movie *The Green Berets* in and around Fort Bragg.

The JFK Special Warfare Museum is free and open to the public from 11:00 A.M. to 4:00 P.M., Tuesday through Sunday. Visitors take note: You used to be able to drive your way unfettered into Fort Bragg to the museum, which is at the corner of Ardennes Road and Marion Street, but recent security measures now require you to pass through a military checkpoint, where your vehicle will be searched. For directions and information about hours and current displays, call (910) 432–4272 or visit www.soc.mil/swcs/museum/museum.shtml.

Go Wild

Fayetteville

Anyone who thinks that Fayetteville is the exclusive terrain of the military hasn't been to Jambbas Ranch, where deer, elk, camels, llamas, buffalo, sheep, rabbits, and other animals have carved out some space of their own.

This natural zoo takes a back-to-basics and refreshingly no-frills approach to putting people inside the animal kingdom. For a minimal price ($6.00 for adults and $4.00 for children, at this writing), you're welcome to wander through the 150-acre preserve. Some of the smaller animals can be petted and fed; others are there just for the watching. Either way, it's a great way to stretch your legs, especially if you wander across the swinging bridge or through the covered one, to mention just two of the place's many unexpected accoutrements.

In 1994 lifelong animal enthusiast Milton Bass opened the ranch, which holds some 400 animals. As much as Bass loves the critters, the retired teacher enjoys introducing them to children, and he has hosted many a student group.

Great ranch, Milton—but what's with the name? It's simple, he'll explain when asked. The name "Jambbas" is an acronym of his wife's and kids' first names: Jimmy, Anna Jean (she's the wife), Milton, Becky, Beth, Anita, and Sabrina.

Jambbas is open every day, weather permitting. Hours are 9:30 A.M. to 5:00 P.M., Monday through Saturday, and 1:00 to 5:00 P.M. on Sunday. To get there, take exit 49 off Interstate 95, go 6 miles east on Highway 53, turn right at Cedar Creek, and go 2 miles on Tabor Church Road. Call (910) 484–4808 or visit www.jambbas.com for more information.

A Babe Is Born
Fayetteville

In 1914 a promising young baseball player, still in his teens, signed up with the Baltimore Orioles, then a minor league outfit. In March of that year, he joined the team for spring training in Fayetteville. It was his first time away from home, and he later marveled about the joy of riding the elevator in the LaFayette Hotel here.

But that was the least of his formative experiences in Fayetteville. At a March 7 game against teammates, he knocked one out of the park—

his first pro-ball home run. As Jim Sumner, a curator at the North Carolina Museum of History, would later note, the hit was "described by Fayetteville residents as the longest home run they had ever seen."

"I hit it as I hit all the others, by taking a good gander at the pitch as it came up to the plate, twisting my body into a backswing, and then hitting it as hard as I could swing," the player who hit that pitch would later explain.

Still, the baby-faced boy was out of his element and clinging to his boss. "He was so inexperienced that, according to legend, one of his teammates saw him tagging along behind [Orioles] manager and owner Jack Dunn in Fayetteville and said, 'There goes Dunn's new babe,'" Sumner recounted.

And that's how George Herman Ruth became "the Babe"—the one and only Babe Ruth. He had a major league contract by the end of the year, and he went on to become one of the men who made the New York Yankees—and baseball, for that matter—a keystone of American sports history. At the peak of his career, Ruth showed his fondness for his home run state, vacationing often in North Carolina, where he traded his bat for a hunting rifle and a set of golf clubs.

"I got to some bigger places than Fayetteville," Ruth would recall in a memoir published shortly before his death in 1948, "but darn few as exciting."

The ball field where Ruth slugged his first high-profile homer is no more, but a state historical marker on nearby Gillespie Street pays permanent tribute to the Babe.

The Long and Wooden Road

Fayetteville

A state full of people on the go, North Carolina sure loves its roads. We'll build 'em anywhere—up and through the sheerest mountain cliffs, above and around coastal waterways, you name it.

And even the ones that cross our flatlands can be somewhat remarkable. Consider for a moment the Fayetteville and Western Plank Road, a wooden construction that was the longest of its type ever built.

It was the 1840s, and state officials were determined to expand and improve North Carolina's long-distance transportation routes. So they hired famed scientist Dr. Elisha Mitchell of the University of North Carolina to study the matter and suggest priority new roads.

To help connect the eastern hub of Fayetteville with points west, Mitchell proposed adopting a relatively novel approach to land travel: so-called "plank roads" made of wood, a material in ready, cheap supply. Building roads from North Carolina's native oak and pine trees, advocates of the idea argued, would prove cheaper than building railroad lines with steel tracks.

Mitchell's idea quickly gained traction, and in 1849 a company formed (with seed money from the state) to build a plank road from Fayetteville to Salisbury. A year later, the first, short stretch opened to public transport.

The 8-foot-wide Fayetteville and Western grew in increments, and for a while it proved to be an expeditious way of traveling on horse- and oxen-drawn coaches and wagons. Every 12 miles or so, there were tollhouses to fund the road's maintenance, but because receipts fell short of the amount needed to build it all the way to Salisbury, the company opted to make Salem the end of the line. Later, the company pushed the road 9 miles north of that town, where it finally ended, 129 miles from its starting point in Fayetteville.

For a time the road was a real economic driver, helping merchants and food and tobacco farmers move their goods and pumping new money into roadside towns and villages along the way. Furniture-manufacturing mecca High Point, for example, "owes its very existence to the wooden highway," as John Hairr noted in the July 2006 issue of *Our State* magazine.

"Unfortunately, the days of prosperity for the Fayetteville and Western were short-lived," Hairr noted. "Few of the road's early advocates had foreseen the high maintenance costs associated with the wooden highway. The heavy flow of traffic quickly wore out the planks, which by necessity had to be replaced, as gaps in the road were extremely hazardous to animals."

In addition, railroads ultimately proved cheaper to maintain, if not to build. The Fayetteville and Western began to fall apart, and when the Civil War began in 1861, it was effectively the end of the road for the world's longest wooden thoroughfare.

Today, the plank roads are noted by—what else?—a historical road marker. It's located on Green Street at Market Square in Fayetteville.

Off the Hook
Grifton

Sadly, for years the little Pitt County town of Grifton had no way to celebrate itself. Then, in 1969, it decided to throw itself a festival. After all, who else would?

Fine, people said, but the festival needs a theme. A man named Ed Comer, then a North Carolina extension agent in town, piped up and said "shad." Well, everybody had a great big chuckle about that one. Shad, they pointed out, were small, bony fish, hardly mascot material. But the town's then-mayor, Dave Bosley, thought that Comer was onto something, pointing out that the festival didn't have to be about *eating* shad; after all, he reasoned, people didn't eat azaleas at the Azalea Festival or mules at Mule Day.

Shad turned out to be a winner, and today the Grifton Shad Festival has survived to become the second-oldest festival in eastern North Carolina. At the five-day event held each April, festivalgoers can play "Shado," an endemic form of bingo; compete in a "Shad Toss" using real (but mercifully dead) fish; browse art stalls; and, if they look hard enough, nibble on bits of shad at a "Here's the Shad" stall. The festival also crowns a Shad Queen and three Shad Princesses.

The Grifton Shad Festival takes its motto from graffiti reading "Eat Mo' Shad" that used to be visible on the bridge spanning Contentnea Creek. That bridge is gone, but you can still see the image on the in-demand T-shirts for sale at the event. People from as far away as Canada have called, positively begging for them. Who can blame them?

For more information, call the Grifton town hall at (252) 524–5168 or visit www.grifton.com. If you can't get enough shad in one day, Greenville, fifteen minutes away, has plenty of lodging options. Grifton is located on Highways 11 and 118, between Kinston and Greenville.

Ironclad

Kinston

Like most nations that fight hard but ultimately lose the war, the Confederate States of America turned in desperation to new technology. The Confederate Navy was outnumbered and outgunned, so—along with swift-moving blockade runners—ironclad gunboats seemed like weapons that could help the underdog separatists turn the tide toward victory.

The Confederate government commissioned twenty-two ironclads, but only one of them still exists today. Well, part of it, at least.

The 158-foot-long CSS *Neuse* played a part in only one battle, late in the war. In March 1865, as Union troops approached Kinston, where the ship was harbored, it was scuttled into the waters of its namesake, the Neuse River—but not before getting off at least a few rounds from its two big guns.

"The ram *Neuse* was destroyed by fire and sunk," wrote a reporter for the *New York Herald* who came into town with the boys in blue. "Her smokestack can be seen now still standing. She must have been a formidable craft."

The CSS *Neuse* needs a hull lot of love.

A century later, what remained of the *Neuse* was recovered, and today a sizable hunk of the hull is on display at the CSS *Neuse* State Historic Site in Kinston, which also hosts an intricate scale model of the craft, complete with a cutaway section to show what the ill-fated iron-clad looked like inside.

The site, at 2612 West Vernon Avenue (U.S. Highway 70 Bus.), is open 9:00 A.M. to 5:00 P.M., Monday through Saturday. Call (252) 522–2091 or visit www.ah.dcr.state.nc.us/sections/hs/neuse/neuse.htm for more information. (And take note: A group formed in the summer of 2006, Friends of the CSS *Neuse,* is raising funds to find a new, climate-controlled building in order to better preserve the ship, so it may soon have a new berth.)

Dude, This Blows

Laurinburg

While many college students busy themselves practicing their charms on the opposite sex, drinking beer, and spending their parents' money, a select few at St. Andrews Presbyterian College spend their time blowing into a leather bladder and making earthy, droning noises. Meet the proud enrollees of one of America's three college-level bagpipe programs.

The unusual course of study is the brainchild of Bill Caudill, director of the school's Scottish Heritage Center and a lifelong player of the Highland pipes. Caudill attended St. Andrews himself and earned a small stipend playing for official events as the school's piper. Now, he shares his skills on this notoriously difficult (and loud) instrument with students.

Some liken playing the bagpipe to "wrestling an octopus." And despite their stirring, martial sound and popularity at solemn occasions, not everyone loves the rustic woodwind instrument.

"They were like, 'What are you thinking?'" said twenty-one-year-old piper Seth Wells of Wilmington, describing his parents' reaction to his newfound passion, in a 2006 Associated Press story. "And it took about a year until I could play without sounding like a dying cat."

Persistence pays off. Or so they say. Regardless, you may want to bring earplugs the next time you're on campus. To acquaint yourself with St. Andrews' Scottish Heritage Center and its piping curriculum, visit www.sapc.edu.

The "Carny Mummy"
Laurinburg

Pity poor Cancetto Farmica. Not so much because of the hardships the Italian immigrant endured while working with a traveling carnival, or even because of the way he perished at the tender age of twenty-three (in 1911 a fellow carny did him in with a tent stake). All that was rough enough, but it was after he died that Farmica endured what might have been the worst indignities.

His body was taken to the McDougald Funeral Home in Laurinburg, where Farmica's father paid $10 to have his son embalmed. He'd be back, he told the funeral director, with money for a proper burial.

But for whatever reason, Farmica's father never returned. So the funeral director made what today might seem an odd decision: He kept the body around, boxed upright in a garage. Over the years the funeral home relocated a few times, taking Farmica along for the ride.

Meanwhile, Farmica's body underwent a kind of mummification—and that's when word spread that the McDougalds had quite the show-and-tell curiosity. In true carnival freak-show fashion, the family let locals come by and have a peek at Farmica, who soon got a nick-name—"Spaghetti"—that was evidently an homage to his country of origin. Lest the moniker seem clichéd or dismissive, old-timers in town are quick to counter that they considered the mummy a treasured, respected member of the community.

Thousands of folks eventually laid eyes on the embalmed Italian American before, in 1972, a U.S. congressman of Italian ancestry, Mario Biaggi of New York, cried foul about the display of Spaghetti's remains. To quell the budding controversy, the McDougalds finally buried Farmica, sixty-one years after that tent stake took him down.

You can still go see Spaghetti (though not exactly the way people once did) at Hillside Cemetery, where he finally rests. To get there, turn west on Hillside Avenue off Business 401 and follow the avenue through the cemetery. Farmica's grave is roadside, close to where the cemetery ends.

Give It a Whirl
Lucama

Some locals call it "acid park," and while the place is truly a trip, it didn't take psychedelic drugs for it to come to be. Instead, it took the persistent efforts of unconventional artist Vollis Simpson—and a whole lot of scrap metal—to put this field full of whirligigs on the map.

"What's a whirligig," you say? A gaze at Simpson's structures offers as good an answer as any, but we'd describe them as colorful, whimsical windmills. The dozens of them that Simpson has installed on his land hang in the air and turn in the breeze, grinding and chiming in a colorful symphony of sight and sound. Together, they are a spectacle that has earned him the description "the Don Quixote of east-central North Carolina."

Simpson, who is now in his mid-eighties, started his "gig" farm in 1985, when he retired from making machines that move houses. Now the machines he makes are more intricate and artful, and they've found their way into many an art exhibit—but they're best viewed at the roadside where he plants them. To get there, take Highway 301 from nearby Wilson, turn right on Wiggins Mill Road, go about 8 miles, and look for the pondside field full of marvelous moving metallica.

Something in the wind: Vollis Simpson's one-of-a-kind creations spin in the breeze.

ROBIN SAGE

To win the right to wear the Green Beret, Army Special Forces trainees must pass through many trials by fire. One of the most important ones, though it's little publicized, is the intensive "qualifying course" known as Robin Sage.

Perhaps the country's longest-running war game, Robin Sage is a two-week guerrilla warfare exercise run out of Fort Bragg since the 1950s that continues to take place in about a dozen neighboring counties four times a year.

There's no live fire—or at least there's not supposed to be—but there are plenty of weapons, and the scenario is crafted to be as real as possible. In the exercise, Special Forces trainees play the part of insurgents rising up against an unpopular, authoritarian government. Over the years local civilians have been enlisted to perform as rebel sympathizers, government informants, and other key roles.

And if it all seems like just a bunch of play-acting, anyone who finds himself or herself in the vicinity of Fort Bragg would do well to remember that war games sometimes play out in an all-too-real fashion.

In February 2002, for example, a Moore County sheriff's deputy shot two soldiers following a roadside stop, killing one of them. The soldiers, who were in civilian garb, reportedly assumed that the law officer was part of the simulation, so they first tried to bribe him with fake money and then to disarm him. The deputy, however, said he was not aware of the army exercise and was forced to defend himself.

Further mishaps followed. In October 2002 four Special Forces trainees broke into the home of an elderly Montgomery County couple, held them at gunpoint, and barked commands at them in Spanish—until the soldiers realized they had targeted the wrong home.

And in February 2005 Robin Sage produced two scares in Asheboro. In the first incident, employees at a local business called the police to report an apparent armed kidnapping—which turned out to be part of the exercise. In the second, two public schools went into lockdown for almost half an hour after staff members spotted armed men near the schools. The men were later identified by army officials as Robin Sage trainees who had evidently not followed their instructions to stay out of sight.

Amid the spate of mishaps, the army has ramped up its effort to make sure local civilians and law enforcement personnel get the word about the quarterly Robin Sage exercises. Consider yourself warned: If you come across a crew-cutted band romping around North Carolina as though they were at war, it's best to believe that they just might think they are.

Live and Learn
Merry Hill

Roger Cullipher was born and raised at Mount Gould, and he grew up with both a wide-ranging interest in the world and a deep appreciation for his own little neck of the woods. As a boy he walked about the fields, finding arrowheads and other Native American artifacts the plow turned up.

Inspired by his experience as a teacher, Cullipher over the years put together the Mount Gould Museum as a destination for students. On display at this modest museum are a number of Native American–themed items, including Cullipher's collection of projectile points as well as a detailed model of a longhouse, files of information on state histories, old woodworking tools, and artifacts from the tobacco and coal industries.

Cullipher was also a gifted craftsman with a touch of whimsy; the collection includes several "footstools" he built—wooden stools whose legs end in leather boots.

The museum is open only by appointment. Call Elaine Taylor at (252) 356–2579 for information. The Mount Gould Museum is located at 137 Mount Gould River Road. Look for the sign on Highway 45.

A Pack Rat to Be Proud Of
Murfreesboro

Usually, obsessive collectors wind up being more of a burden than a boon. An old aunt and uncle, say, who kept everything they ever came across—and left their family to deal with all the stuff when they passed to the possession-less afterlife.

That certainly wasn't the case with Brady C. Jefcoat of Raleigh, who bequeathed a mother lode of goodies that we can all delight in at the Brady C. Jefcoat Museum.

Jefcoat's collections are justly described on the town of Murfreesboro's Web site as "overwhelming"—but in the best way possible. He assembled a century's worth (roughly 1850–1950) of American cultural and industrial artifacts that together defy easy description. Suffice it say that visitors encounter rooms full of air rifles, music boxes, phonographs, stuffed animals (the taxidermied kind), unconventional furniture, vintage washing machines, and much, much more.

"You really have to see to believe it," Murfreesboro's Web site claims, and it's hard to argue with that.

The museum, which is housed in the historic Mufreesboro High School building at 201 West High Street, is open from 11:00 A.M. to 4:00 P.M. on Saturday and 2:00 to 5:00 P.M. on Sunday. For more information call (252) 398–5922 or visit www.murfreesboronc .com/historic/tour/jefcoat .htm.

Nurse!: Few places can boast a collection of bedpans to rival the Jefcoat Museum's.

A Little Golf, Anyone?

Pinehurst

Mention miniature golf today, and for many folks it will call to mind little more than a campy amusement. But that wasn't always the case.

In fact, there was a time when minigolf was nothing short of a class act—a diversion reserved for the upper crust. And it all started in Pinehurst, which today is a full-size golfing mecca.

Meet putting pioneer James Barber, an avid gardener and golfer who wasn't afraid to think small. In 1916 he constructed an artfully reduced version of his favorite sport with eighteen holes and all the flourishes of a classically landscaped garden. Today, his creation is justly remembered as the "first quintessential miniature golf course."

Barber chose the Tuileries Garden next to the Louvre in Paris as his model, and stuck close enough to it to garner national attention here. His intricate neoclassical design included fountains, ornate planters, and symmetrical paths from hole to hole.

When Barber's minilinks were completed, he's said to have looked over the grounds, nodded, and said approvingly, "This'll do."

And so the putting course got an appropriately Scottish-sounding name, Thistle Dhu. Today, the course is long gone, appearing only in obscure histories of minigolf, a sport that can accurately—and proudly, we might add—be called both marginal and popular.

Thistle Dhu set off a nationwide craze. In the 1920s minigolf became a leisure fad, as the tiny courses sprang up in such rarified locales as Manhattan rooftops. By the 1930s thousands of the courses were established around the nation, providing cheap enjoyment even during the dark days of the Great Depression. Barber's dream to bring golf down to size had become a permanent part of the country's curious reality.

So the next time you're aiming a ball into a pint-size windmill or fiberglass dinosaur's mouth, think of Barber, who can justly be called the father of minigolf. And when you sink a hole in one, say what he'd say: "This'll do."

My, How Things Have Changed

Red Springs

Most every town has its museum, and most of them are consigned to recording a history that may not hold much charm for anyone outside of the town limits. The Red Springs Historical Museum is an exception. It manages to break the mold a bit, displaying both mundane and off-the-wall memorabilia.

On the mundane side, the museum displays antique bottles and the plans for the town's post office, among other items.

On the more exotic side, it features a small but shocking exhibition of lightning rods, a section dedicated to the various types of barbed wire used through the ages, and the restored beauty of a local beauty shop.

From Red Springs to the moon: local astronaut William McArthur's NASA uniform.

211

Then there's the "What am I?" exhibit, which is aptly described on a state history Web site as a place "in which formerly commonplace, now obscure everyday items are displayed without labels and visitors can try to identify each item and its use." And don't forget to take in the display on William S. McArthur, a Red Springs native who made his name as an astronaut.

The museum is located at 217 South Main Street. Call (910) 843–4654 for the latest on exhibits and hours.

Sphere of Influence
Rocky Mount

No one in Rocky Mount seems to know where Thelonious S. Monk Park is located, and maybe that's OK. The municipal park was renamed for the jazz great in 2000, and it's possible the new distinction just hasn't sunk in yet.

The man should have a park, at the very least. Monk (whose middle name was Sphere) is likely the most famous native son of this Nash County city, which is perched at the fall line between the state's Piedmont and Coastal Plain.

Born in 1919, Monk lived in Rocky Mount until he was age nine, when his family moved to New York City. The young pianist honed his chops in a traveling gospel outfit, went on to anchor the rhythm section of a number of big bands, and then, in the 1940s, along with trumpeter Dizzy Gillespie and saxophonist Charlie Parker, gave birth to the style called bebop, which dominated the sound of jazz until the early 1960s.

As a pianist, Monk was known for his off-center accompaniment, his shimmering runs across the keyboard, and his odd dissonances and quirky harmonies. He was a prolific composer, writing scores of original tunes—"Blue Monk" and "'Round Midnight" are among his best-known ones—and had a way of beating even the most tired jazz and Tin Pan Alley melodies into something fresh and engaging.

Thelonious S. Monk Park is located south of downtown Rocky Mount, past the warehouse district and nestled inside a city housing project. Neighbors of the park still call it Wye Park for the road that leads up to it, ending in a cul-de-sac.

We visited at dusk on a hot summer evening and found little to see—a few young people playing basketball on a nearby court, some picnic tables, and the park's sign, of course, which sits in a broad expanse of wiregrass. This modest park is the only civic monument we're aware of dedicated to this giant of American music.

Beyond his musical brilliance Monk was known for the strange hats he wore and his habit of rising between solos to dance ecstatically. His namesake park might not inspire you to do the same, but it's better, perhaps, than nothing at all.

To get there, take Washington Street out of downtown Rocky Mount and turn right on Wye Street. The park is free to the public. For more information call (252) 972–1153.

Thelonious Monk first tickled the keys in Rocky Mount.

He made his name in New York City, but

Ava Gardner Museum
Smithfield

Tom Banks was starstruck by Ava Gardner before Hollywood had ever heard of her. He was ten years old when Gardner, then taking secretarial classes at Atlantic Christian College in Wilson, favored the lucky boy with a peck on the cheek.

One kiss was all it took, and Banks was to become a lifelong fan of the woman who got her first casting call a year later, in 1941. Gardner, who was born in Smithfield in 1922, gained fame as one of the great, graceful stars of her time.

When he grew up, Banks corresponded with Gardner and struck up a lasting friendship with her, even serving as the publicist for one of her films. And he developed a true fan's obsession with the actress, collecting every scrap of Gardner-related material he could get his hands on.

By the time he was done, the collection could have fetched a pretty penny at auction. But rather than sell it, Banks paid Gardner the ultimate tribute: In 1981 he bought a building in Smithfield where the actress had lived as a child, renovated it, and made his collection the core of the Ava Gardner Museum. Years later, his material was supplemented with a donation from a fellow Gardner-phile, Dutch artist Bert Pfeiffer.

The museum features an impressive array of well-preserved memorabilia—costumes, vintage movie posters and magazines, portraits, thousands of studio photos, and more—spanning Gardner's life and career. There's even a watch she gave her onetime husband, Frank Sinatra.

Each fall, the museum plays host to the Ava Gardner Fest, a celebration that includes screenings of the actress's classic films, jazz concerts, and other highlights.

After a career that took her around the world, Gardner chose Smithfield as her resting place. She's buried in a family plot at Sunset Memorial Park.

The museum, at 325 East Market Street in downtown Smithfield, is open from 9:00 A.M. to 5:00 P.M. Monday through Saturday and from 2:00 to 5:00 P.M. on Sunday. Admission ranges from $3.00 to $5.00. Call (919) 934–5830 for more details, or make a virtual visit at www.avagardner.org.

Smithfield was proud of Ava Gardner, and she was proud of Smithfield.

Hamming It Up
Smithfield

If you visit the annual Ham & Yam Festival, it pays to bring your appetite. Smithfield is famous for its pigs—and to a lesser degree, its sweet potatoes—and both can be had in just about any form.

The festival, which is held in early May and celebrated its twenty-second anniversary in 2006, is a multifaceted affair focused on food and fun. On the food front the festival features a ham-cooking contest, a sweet potato pie–eating contest, and even a potato-decorating contest for the younger set (which goes by the name "What's That Yam Thing?").

And aside from all the down-home edibles, there's plenty of entertainment, from live music to a classic car show to pig races. The festival, to put it plainly, is nothing to oink at.

For more on the Ham & Yam Festival, call (919) 934–0887 or visit www.downtownsmithfield.com.

The Wonder of It All
Southern Pines

The Taxidermy Hall of Fame of North Carolina Creation Museum and Antique Tool Museum endeavors to display the scope of God's handiwork here on earth with a slew of mounted and stuffed animals. There are more than 200 specimens from the animal kingdom in lifelike poses, along with things generally less associated with the Almighty, such as golf balls, coils of barbed wire, an array of antique can openers, and hundreds of carpentry tools.

That the museum doesn't quite know what it is suits us just fine. In fact, it makes the place infinitely more interesting than it otherwise might be.

All the false gods you can fit in a display cabinet.

The museum and an associated Christian bookstore are located inside an unassuming storefront at 156 N.W. Broad Street. Follow signs from US 1 to downtown Southern Pines. Hours are 9:00 A.M. to 5:00 P.M., Monday through Saturday. Call (910) 692–3471 for more information.

A Bellow from Way Back

Spivey's Corner

Before the cell phone, the pager, the land-line, before the telegraph and even the tin-cans-and-string combination, there was hollerin'. Among rural arts it was the loudest, best way to get the attention of a neighbor, either in time of need or simply to ask, "How you?"

Every year since 1969, hollerers have descended on the small crossroads town of Spivey's Corner to bust their lungs at the National Hollerin' Contest. The event has grown from a modest showcase of local talent to an international phenomenon. Past winners have strutted their stuff on the *David Letterman Show*, *Good Morning America*, and *Regis and Kathy Lee*.

Hollers are hard to define. They are highly variable, taking the form of stylized chicken calls, hoots, otherworldly warbles, the baying of hounds, and wide-open Tarzanesque bellows. Some contestants even deliver sacred hollers such as "Amazing Grace." Old-timers have names for particular styles of the vocal gymnastics, like the "run holler," a continuous moan said to carry far and well on the still air of late afternoon.

Beyond its appeal as a relic of former times, the holler just might have currency in our modern world, according to at least one aficionado. "I'm a-tell you how you can stay strong and live long," one contestant said a few years back. "Holler on a regular basis. Think about it—back when hollering was goin' on people wasn't goin' to psychologists and takin' all this nerve medicine." The message is simple. Save on antidepressants: Holler.

The National Hollerin' contest attracts thousands to Spivey's Corner, albeit temporarily. Proceeds from the one-day event, which also includes a conch-blowin' contest, tasty barbecue, and plenty of craft vendors, benefit the Spivey Corner Volunteer Fire Department.

For more information call the Spivey's Corner VFD at (910) 567–2600 or visit www.hollerincontest.com. Spivey's Corner is located at the crossroads of Highway 13 and Highway 421 between Dunn and Clinton. It's fifteen minutes from the Dunn exit on Interstate 95 and twenty minutes from I–40.

Just Ducky

Weldon

It's official—the rubber duck race has proved itself to be an idea that floats.

Each year, more than one hundred locales across the country host ducky races for this or that charity. Here's how it works: Citizens put up a nominal sum to sponsor a rubber ducky that is entered into a race down some local waterway. The first few to drift across the finish line earn their sponsors some prize money; the rest of the funds go to a good local cause.

And so it goes in Weldon, home to what is apparently North Carolina's largest duck race. In August 2006 the town hosted the fourteenth annual Ducky Derby, sending hundreds of the rubber toys down the Roanoke River to raise cash for the Roanoke Valley Chamber of Commerce and area Smart Start programs.

Five dollars will get your duck in the race, and whether or not you compete, there's plenty of music, food, and crafts on hand for festivalgoers. Local businesses can also compete to see who can best decorate a wooden duck.

For information about next August's Ducky Derby, which will certainly be something to quack about, call (252) 537–3513.

The "Two-Headed Nightingale"
Whiteville

North Carolina has been blessed with some of the most remarkable conjoined twins to ever walk this world. Chang and Eng Bunker, originally from Siam, settled near Mount Airy and achieved worldwide acclaim. The Hilton sisters traveled from fame to obscurity before settling in Charlotte. But let us not forget the powerful pair known as Millie-Christine McCoy—two hearts, two voices, and one incredible saga.

The two were born to slave parents in 1851. Their bodies were conjoined, and they were enough of a physical anomaly that profiteers immediately seized on the chance to display them. Sold to a showman as infants, they were shortly thereafter kidnapped by another promoter and shipped to England. Eventually, they were retrieved and brought home to the United States, where they toured with P. T. Barnum's circus.

Millie-Christine, the "two-headed nightingale."

Along the way Millie-Christine carved out what now seems a perplexing identity: In many ways they considered themselves one person, and were marketed as such. To this day "they" are often referred to as "she" or "her"—as a single individual.

But although they were joined by the closest of bonds, they *were* two people, and together they cultivated extraordinary talents. They learned to speak five languages, play music, and dance, and they joined their voices in song with such skill that they became known as "The Two-Headed Nightingale." Performing for such world leaders as Queen Victoria—who bestowed them with jewelry in appreciation for their music—they were also touted as "The Eighth Wonder of the World."

The twins died in 1912 from tuberculosis. Over the following decades their unique story slowly faded away. Fortunately, in 2000 writer Joanne Martell published the first comprehensive biography, *Millie-Christine: Fearfully and Wonderfully Made,* giving the sisters their historical due.

Millie and Christine are buried in the Welches Creek Community Cemetery, their second resting place (their remains were moved in 1969 from an overgrown, near-forgotten plot). A stone marker reads, in part, "A soul with two thoughts. Two hearts that beat as one."

THE TIDEWATER

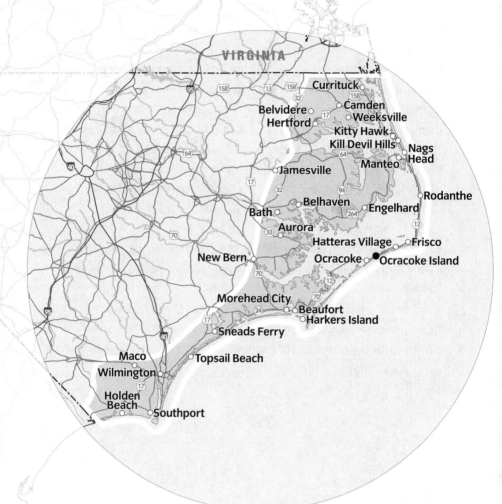

VIRGINIA

Currituck
Camden
Belvidere
Weeksville
Hertford
Kitty Hawk
Kill Devil Hills
Nags Head
Jamesville
Manteo
Rodanthe
Belhaven
Engelhard
Bath
Aurora
Frisco
Hatteras Village
New Bern
Ocracoke
Ocracoke Island
Morehead City
Beaufort
Harkers Island
Sneads Ferry
Maco
Topsail Beach
Wilmington
Holden Beach
Southport

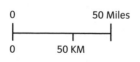

0   50 Miles

0   50 KM

THE TIDEWATER

North Carolina's easternmost province is a watery place, full of broad rivers and sounds, and ending at the mighty, heaving Atlantic Ocean.

Little surprise, then, that many of its distinctions are more than a little blue: the lives of the famous pirates, living and dead, the wrecks of ships fated to fetch on our Tar Heel shores, the graves of lost sailors, and the dugout canoes the state's original residents used to run their errands in.

We cast our nets wide for treasures, and came up with some notable places to visit. At Aurora, for instance, if you're brave enough, you can slip your head inside the jaws of a giant, prehistoric shark. At Nags Head, you can gaze on the wonders of one woman's lifetime of beach-combing. Feeling hungry? At Jamesville you can put away a bubbling platter of oily fish like gastronomes of old.

True, there are other funky treasures that don't have the faintest whiff of the sea about them: in Belhaven, a woman's lifetime collection of buttons; near Elizabeth City, a building big enough to hide a blimp; at Engelhard, a house with eight sides, and at Holden Beach, a true-believer's yard-decorating scheme that at once brings glory to the Almighty and brings food to struggling children around the world.

We say that's a mighty big bunch of stuff to see. Now, if you'll allow us, we'll point you in the right direction . . .

THIS PLACE IS A WRECK

Seafaring and the Outer Banks have been a deadly mix since at least the sixteenth century, when the English ship *Tyger* went down here. Things only got worse in following centuries, and, thanks to the Banks' storms and capricious shoals (and an unwanted boost from German U-boats), records indicate that as many as 2,000 ships have made their permanent home in these waters—namely, on the bottom.

In most parts of the world, if you want to view shipwrecks, you're out of luck unless you're scuba-certified. Not so here in the "graveyard of the Atlantic," where a handful of ships' hulks are visible and, in a few cases, even touchable.

Here are several, listed from north to south:

- The schooner *Francis E. Waters*, which sank in October 1889, is on display on the lawn at the Nags Head town hall. You hardly have to get out of your car to feel the fear.
- The schooner *Laura A. Barnes*, which sank in June 1921, sits between the dunes at Coquina Beach in the Cape Hatteras National Seashore.
- The trawler *Lois Joyce*, which sank December 1981, is from time to time visible in the surf at Oregon Inlet.
- The Union transport *Oriental* sank in May 1862. Today, her boiler stack—a bulbous, black structure—is visible from the second beach access past the Oregon Inlet Bridge.

The *Francis E. Waters* has come to rest outside the Nags Head Town Hall.

- An unknown but nonetheless unfortunate barge can be seen at low tide directly across from the U.S. Fish and Wildlife Service station, just north of Rodanthe.
- What's left of the schooner *Altoona*, which sank in 1878, is visible just north of the pond at Cape Point, Buxton.

If you just can't get enough of the Outer Banks's historic misfortune and mayhem, a host of downed ships' nameplates are on display at the Chicamacomico Life Saving Station in Rodanthe.

Supersize Me

Aurora

Talk about your tough neighborhoods. Fifty million years ago, the seas off what today is North Carolina were brimming with sharks that grew nearly three times as long as the average great white shark does today. *Carcharocles megalodon* measured up to 52 feet and had individual teeth that were bigger than a man's hand. The monumental fish is believed to have been the second-largest predator ever to live, after today's sperm whale.

In fact, almost everything—except, perhaps, the national debt—was bigger in former times. To get a look at some of these outsize remains from the Eocene Epoch through the modern era, pay a call to the Aurora Fossil Museum.

When engineers first started using machines to chew into the vast deposits of mineral phosphate in eastern Beaufort County, layer by layer they revealed a history of the ancient world. They found trilobites, echinoids, and things with still odder names.

Jurassic shark! If you're hungry for ancient history, the Aurora Fossil Museum will satisfy.

Inside the museum is displayed a Pleistocene Age walrus skull that was dredged off the coast of North Carolina and a 20-million-year-old fossil whale skeleton. The Shark Room has a wall of jaws from the feared fish, with comparisons of modern and primitive sharks. There is even a replica *C. megalodon* jaw, inside which visitors can have their pictures taken, smiling nervously. Outside, a constantly replenished fossil pit allows visitors to dig for their very own piece of ancient history.

Aurora is located at the junction of Routes 33 and 206 in Beaufort County. The museum address is 400 Main Street. Call (252) 322–4238 or visit www.aurorafossilmuseum.com for more information. The museum is free and open seven days a week.

Hell of a Way to Go
Bath

People in Bath don't cotton to Sunday horse races, and rightfully so. Just ask them about Jesse Elliott.

At the beginning of the nineteenth century, the Bath native was a notorious hell-raiser who had an appetite for pursuing equestrian sports on the Lord's Day. (*Note:* bad idea.) One Sunday morning, Elliott was the odds-on favorite in a race when his horse bucked and threw him against a pine tree. The tree didn't give much, and Elliott was killed instantly, going immediately from tough-guy status to cautionary tale.

But the really chilling thing about Elliott's demise was the last thing he uttered before he left this world for the next: "Take me in a winner or take me to hell."

Of course, a tale grew up around Elliott's death so big that it included a mysterious "dark rider" (the Devil) and other questionable embellishments. Yet the fact remains that today in Bath there exist mysterious hoofprints that people insist were made by the horse Elliott rode during his final, deadly race.

A LOVER AND A FIGHTER

History's revisionists tell us that Edward Teach, aka Blackbeard, was as misunderstood as he was fierce. By the new measure Teach was just another enterprising guy trying to get along under the iron fist of the British crown.

In 1718, feeling a little weary from his high-seas skirmishes, the fabled pirate had his own "summer of love." Legend has it that he sailed up the Pamlico River nearly to Bath and, at Plum Point, about a mile below the town, built a house for the young love who would become his thirteenth bride. The point, with its wide view of Bath Creek, was not just a romantic outpost but also a good place for a wanted man to keep an eye out for the law.

The two lived there for just a season. By summer's end, after wining and dining his new bride, Blackbeard was restless and broke. The pull of the sea, and piracy, by extension, proved too much for him. Although we can't know exactly what he said to his betrothed, it was probably something along the lines of "Later, 'gator." With that, Blackbeard was gone.

By November Teach was dead, having suffered twenty-five wounds during a pitched shipboard battle with Lieutenant Robert Maynard and a slew of British naval officers off Ocracoke Island. The guy was hard to kill, and little wonder, if you take this passage from

Charles Johnson's *A General History of the Pyrates,* published in London in 1726, for truth:

> [His] Beard was black, which he suffered to grow of an extravagant Length; as to Breadth, it came up to his Eyes; he was accustomed to twist it with Ribbons, in small Tails . . . and turn them about his Ears: In Time of Action, he wore a sling over his Shoulders, with three Brace of Pistols, hanging in Holsters like Bandaliers; and stuck lighted Matches under his Hat, which appearing on each Side of his Face, his Eyes naturally looking fierce and wild, made him altogether such a Figure, that Imagination cannot form an Idea of a Fury, from Hell, to look more frightful.

Hell, yes, but clearly Teach had a more tender side. And what of his lonely bride? Her story is lost to us.

Meanwhile, at Plum Point, archaeologists have uncovered a foundation as well as bits of English pottery through several decades of searching. But there is no conclusive evidence linking the area to Edward Teach, or the treasure chest, bristling with gold doubloons, he purportedly buried here. Nevertheless, people still come here to swat at mosquitoes and get caught up in the allure of one of history's baddest, lovin'-est dudes.

Artifacts from a ship believed to be *Queen Anne's Revenge,* one of Blackbeard's earlier vessels, are on display at the North Carolina Maritime Museum at Beaufort (www.ah.dcr.state.nc.us/section/maritime).

Despite the fact that the impressions were made in loamy soil more than two centuries ago, no vegetation grows in or around them. Or so people say. Today, the prints are on private property, and you risk trespassing if you go looking for them.

Nevertheless, there they are, along Goose Creek State Park Road, off U.S. Highway 264, a mute reminder of why today Down Easters don't race horses on Sunday. If you're inclined to hunt them up, you'd better ask permission or risk joining Jesse Elliott in the Bad Place. Don't say we didn't warn you.

Shiver Me Timbers!

Beaufort

Captain Horatio Sinbad was born Ross Morphew in Detroit, Michigan. When he was but a wee lad of ten, he watched Walt Disney's adaptation of Robert Louis Stevenson's *Treasure Island* swashbuckling across his family's TV screen, and his fate was more or less sealed. He was certain that he would grow up to be a pirate.

It took some doing. A pirate is nothing without a boat, so the young Morphew started building one in his father's workshop. A year later, he finished it. Five years after that, he set off for a year to serve as a crewman on sailing craft in the Caribbean. A fellow sailor gave him a nickname that stuck: Sinbad.

Morphew returned home tanned and inspired, and he started work on a 22-foot sailboat he named the *Meka I*. He sailed it toward St. Lucia on his honeymoon and into the teeth of a hurricane. The boat sank. Thankfully, he and his bride were rescued by a passing freighter.

Back in Detroit again—spirits bruised but his love of sail undiminished—he started work on a second, bigger vessel, the *Meka II*. When completed, it was 54 feet long and built along the lines of a seventeenth century brigantine.

In 1970 Morphew finally abandoned the landlubber's life altogether for one of adventure on the high seas. He and his wife split amicably. (The breakup may or may not have had something to do with his decision to legally change his name to Horatio Sinbad.)

Sinbad sailed the *Meka II* south and found a favorable berth in Beaufort, where he remains to this day. A grizzled, big-bearded specimen of a man, Captain Sinbad in 2002 sailed his ship to an unlikely blood-and-sweat victory in the Americas' Sail Class B race, held in Jamaica. In a June 2006 article in *Our State* magazine, Sinbad explained to writer L. A. Jackson the secret behind the triumph: "We took off, and we were sailing everything—bunk sheets, bikini tops, boxer shorts—everything. And that's how we won."

Recognizing a real, live (not to mention *swashbuckling*) state treasure in his midst, Governor Michael Easley granted Sinbad a privateer's commission in 2005. (It was that or walk the plank.)

Go ahead and pay Cap'n Sinbad a call, ye scurvy dogs—iffin' ye dare. But first, visit his Web site (every successful pirate has one) at www.pirate-privateer.com and learn a little more about this modern-day buccaneer.

A pirate's life for he: Horatio Sinbad sails in Blackbeard's wake.

Super Saver

Belhaven

A thumbnail sketch provided by the August 17, 1951, *Washington Daily News* described Mrs. Mary Eva Blount Way ("Miss Eva" to those who knew her) as "a housewife, snakekiller, curator, trapper, dramatic actress, philosopher, and preserver of all the riches of mankind," but added that those descriptors "inadequately describe the most fascinating person you can imagine."

But the most remarkable thing about Miss Eva was the fact that she never threw anything away, beginning with a handful of prized buttons her mother-in-law gave her as a young bride. She called it her "vitamins," this habit of collecting. From a lifetime of holding onto things, here is a sampling of some of the things she accumulated: Civil War relics, a World War I German spiked helmet inscribed MIT GOTT FUR KOENIG UND VATERLAND (with God for king and country), petrified walrus tusks, a human skull, a three-legged pig, whale bones, a flea wedding (bride and groom fleas in full wedding regalia, with magnifying glass to aid viewing), clothing of former times, a watch fashioned from the first Atlantic cable, and about 30,000 buttons.

Beginning in 1940, when she was seventy-one years old, Way's collection was on view at her house near Belhaven. The exhibit was free, but visitors were encouraged to leave a donation for worthy causes such as the Red Cross. When the number of things in the collection surpassed 10,000, a nearby barn was brought into service as additional storage.

When Way died in 1962 at age ninety-three, Belhaven residents made sure the collection passed into civic hands. Today, Miss Eva's stuff is on display in the upstairs of the town hall. It's called "Granny's Attic."

Way was fond of saying that "hobbies are wonderful cures for all ills." Judging from the amazing contents of her museum, Miss Eva must have been a very healthy woman indeed.

The Belhaven Memorial Museum is open daily except for Wednesday. Admission is free, but donations are encouraged. The museum is located on East Main Street (Business 264) on the second floor of the old town hall. Belhaven is 30 miles east of Washington on U.S. Highway 264. Call (252) 943–6817 for more information.

Got a bone to pick? How about a state made of buttons? The unexpected —and lots of it—at the Belhaven Memorial Museum.

Quake, Rattle, and Roll
Belvidere

In the late 1600s members of the Protestant denomination known as the Quakers founded a new community in Perquimans County. They called it Belvidere. Quakers were known for their moderation and plainness of dress, so it may seem a slight incongruity that the home of one of Belvidere's upstanding Quakers came to be the dwelling place of one of rock 'n' roll's wild men.

In 1989 radio legend Robert W. "Wolfman Jack" Smith bought Thomas Newby's Belvidere Plantation, built in 1785, and lived there until his death from a heart attack in 1995. His wife, Lou Lamb, was a Belvidere native.

Smith was born in 1938 in Brooklyn, New York, and began his radio career at Newport News, Virginia, in 1960. Over a three-decade career, he played rock 'n' roll, rhythm and blues, gospel, and the occasional country song at stations from Virginia to Los Angeles to border stations in Mexico.

His autobiography, *Have Mercy! Confessions of the Original Rock 'n' Roll Animal*, was released shortly before his death. In it Smith wrote that "being the Wolfman is more than just spinning records and making a funky, beastly sound of joy come out of a human throat. It's being a mouthpiece for the possibility of happiness, it's about the great connection to humanity that you can find in just spreading love around and being your own true self."

An appearance in the 1973 film *American Graffiti* helped revive Smith's flagging career and bring him back from a decade of hard-partying ways.

Another passage from his book, full of the rapid-fire rapping he was known for, is a fitting epitaph for the famed deejay. "No matter if you're feeling happy or depressed, come on in here man," he wrote. "We're going to fill you with a little goodness. Maybe you're under a dark cloud. Well, there's a bright, sunshiny day over here. . . . We're gonna cook a big pot of that Memphis Soul Stew until we do a total re-do on your boogaloo situation."

Belvidere Plantation remains a private residence and is not open to the public, but the gravel-throated deejay's grave is visible from the road here. Perquimans County has organized a driving tour of the Belvidere Historic District, with other Quaker landmarks for the viewing. For more information, call (252) 426–5657 or visit the county's Chamber of Commerce, located at 118 West Market Street in Hertford.

Pump It Up

Camden

Mace Quidley has a gas problem: He can't get enough of gasoline pumps—the older and more unconventional the better.

It may seem an odd obsession to average Americans, most of whom make their pit stops as perfunctory as possible. But for Quidley, who once worked at a service station and today maintains Quidley's General Store as a private museum, gas pumps fuel the fire of a bona fide obsession. For him gas gear is, well, a gas.

"It's just amazing to me that there are so many different kinds, different shapes and different colors," he told *Our State* magazine in 2006. As a guy who stores more than sixty models in his backyard, he should know. He lovingly restores them—to what end, we're not exactly sure.

But love them he does, especially the more unique varieties. He described a 1915 model to *Our State* in anatomical terms. "Collectors call it the Mae West pump," he noted, "I guess because it's real big at the bottom, skinny in the middle and big at the top."

In an age when fossil fuels seem to be on the wane (and potentially the bane of our existence, for that matter), somehow there's something poignant about a fellow who's intent on preserving the relics of many a road trip.

Quidley, we should mention, is not singularly obsessed with gas pumps. "You name, I collect it," he says. A one-man preservation squad, his collection includes everything from old jukeboxes to vintage oil cans to antique cars. "Every time I think I have it all," he told one reporter, "I go out and find something else."

Incarceration Station

Currituck

The town of Currituck (population 700) is a small, blink-and-you'll-miss-it place, but it has at least one major distinction: its jail.

The Jacobean-style brick building measures only about 20 by 30 feet—hardly SuperMax dimensions—but it's one of the oldest, if not *the* oldest, jail in North Carolina.

Currituck was first settled in 1668 and immediately became one of the state's most important ports. Of course ports are known to attract a certain kind of person, and, by the early 1700s, the county fathers saw fit to bring justice here by building a courthouse. Not long after, the colonial legislature granted permission for the construction of a jail. The current structure is believed to date from 1790.

The name Currituck is an Algonquian Indian word meaning "the land of the wild goose," in recognition of all the waterfowl attracted to the county's marshes during the winter months. Tough luck to be in the Currituck clink and, just beyond the walls, to hear the honking of geese and keening of swans, footloose and fancy-free.

The jail is now the registrar's office and is open from 9:00 A.M. to 5:00 P.M., Monday through Friday. However, no public tours are available. It's located just off Highway 158, near the Knott's Island Ferry landing.

A Heady House
Engelhard

Phrenology—the art of divining a person's personality, character, and moral development from the shape of his or her head—was never more popular than during the nineteenth century. When he wasn't fondling people's heads, Orson S. Fowler, one of that century's leading phrenologists, was putting his architectural skills to work in service of the eight-sided house.

In the 1850s Fowler, whose phrenology practice was located in New York City, wrote a book called *The Octagon House, A Home for All.* His designs had wide influence and, for a short while, constituted a fad.

Eight is enough at Engelhard's Octagon House.

One of these houses stands today near Engelhard, in Hyde County. Built in 1857, the Octagon House—or "round house" or "inkpot house," as it is variously called—has its roots in Fowler's design. The house was built by Dr. William T. Sparrow, a physician and phrenologist himself. Sparrow was born in Craven County but later married a Hyde County woman. The Octagon House has two stories, wood floors, and four fireplaces connected to a central chimney. Each level has six rooms and a central hall. The house has no posts, except at the windows and door.

Only two octagonal houses dating from the nineteenth century still stand in North Carolina. The design never really took off. Why is anybody's guess: Maybe they lacked the coziness of a bungalow or a simple frame house. Maybe owners disliked the fact that it was hard to get away from their spouse and kids in a house that had no corners. Who knows? We can only speculate, like a phrenologist feeling for telltale bumps.

A group called Octagon House Restoration Inc. maintains the house and, money allowing, plans to do a full restoration of it. Each year a Christmas open house is held here. For hours and tour information, call Partnership for the Sound at (252) 796–3008.

The Octagon House is located off U.S. Highway 264 south of Engelhard.

Take Us to Your Leader

Frisco

The future is visible on Hatteras Island near Frisco, just east of a straightaway on Highway 12. Behold: the silver skin, the stilt legs, the alien faces peering from ellipsoid windows. Surrounded by weeds and rusted trucks, the spaceship looks a little out of place, like a prop flown off the set of *Lost in Space* only to touch down later on Planet *Sanford and Son.*

What you're seeing is the Outer Banks's only Futuro house, a roadside attraction reckoned by some to be Hatteras Island's second-most-photographed landmark after its famous candy-striped lighthouse.

Frisco's Futuro House—an extraterrestrial home makeover.

Greenville resident Jim Bagwell currently owns the house, which first landed on Hatteras in 1970. In its time the pod has seen use as an oceanfront cottage, a Boy Scout meeting place, a short-lived magazine's office, a hot dog stand, and a knickknack shop. Back when it was located in Hatteras Village, surfers used the dune-mounted spaceship to gauge their proximity to a favorite sandbar.

It continues to exert a magnetic attraction on the island's nearly one million annual visitors.

"It definitely triggers something in people," Bagwell says. "For me, it's the sort of spaceship I grew up with back in the 1950s."

Futuro houses were designed by Finnish architect Matti Suuronen in the mid-1960s. A prototype made of fiberglass and polyurethane foam was unveiled in 1968. Its built-in furnishings included a central living area with six chairs that could be converted into beds, a central fireplace/grill, a bathroom, and a kitchenette. An airplane-style folding staircase provided entry to the house.

Today, the houses are as rare as moon rocks. No more than a hundred were made during their entire production run, which lasted until the late 1970s, and estimates place the remaining number somewhere between a dozen and sixty.

Since he bought it five years ago, Bagwell says he's received "innumerable" offers to buy the spaceship, but he's holding firm, still scheming new plans for it.

"I've thought I could maybe open a hamburger stand in it, call it 'Out of This World Hamburgers,' you know, or something like that."

For now the spaceship remains a vacant but irresistible curiosity, and the patch of naked sand in front of it attests to the number of drive-bys it receives. Hang around it on a summer day, and you'll see vehicles with plates from Quebec to Florida slow and then stop beside the Futuro. Carloads of visitors will get out, swat at a few mosquitoes, pose to have their pictures taken beside it, and then drive on.

Bagwell enjoys all the attention but admits having one regret: "If I'd found a way to charge a dollar for every picture taken of the thing," he laments, "I'd be retired by now."

The Futuro house is located on the east (ocean) side of Highway 12 in Frisco. It's hard to miss.

Going Native

Frisco

Carl Bornfriend took an interest in Native American life decades before *Dances with Wolves* was a twinkle in some producer's eye. Where others were indifferent to the handiworks of North America's first residents, Bornfriend was awed.

In the 1980s Bornfriend moved to the Outer Banks and met his now-wife, Joyce. The two were teachers and saw the educational value of Bornfriend's pet passion. In their spare time they began turning a former village store into a museum.

WEAVING
RUG: NAVAJO
"EYE DAZZLER"
DON'T STARE AT THIS RUG!!

This means you: Friendly advice at the Frisco Native American Museum.

241

In 1987 they opened it as the Frisco Native American Museum. The rambling, one-story building is full of treasures depicting the life of "the first peoples" through history and across the continent, including spear points, textiles, peace tokens offered to tribes by emissaries from the United States, mounted animals, and even a dugout canoe discovered on-site. The museum offers a wealth of information, made all the more impressive by the fact that it was created out of passion and private funds.

The Frisco Native American Museum is located on the west side of Highway 12 in Frisco. It is open daily from 11:00 A.M. to 5:00 P.M. Call (252) 995–4440 or visit www.nativeamericanmuseum.org for more information, including current admission prices.

Duck, Duck, Goose
Harkers Island

Duck hunting once was big business along North Carolina's coast. Birds would flock by the millions to the coastal sounds beginning in late fall, to overwinter in the relatively mild conditions with ample food for the dabbling. When they reached the temperate southern waters from their Canadian summer haunts, hunters were there to greet them with guns a-blazin'.

In the late nineteenth century, as the nation's Northeast grew and became urbanized, these "market gunners" bagged birds by the thousands and filled barrels with them for shipment to fine restaurants in New York, Philadelphia, and Boston. Market gunners' technology was refined to include small skiffs mounted with "punt guns"—giant shotguns that could be loaded with most anything sharp or deadly.

The hunters' work was not all buckshot and explosions, though. In fact, it was part art: During the off-season, they spent hours carving blocks of native wood into realistic decoys that could be floated on the water to lure in their unsuspecting quarry.

Today, hundreds of decoys are on display at the Core Sound Waterfowl Museum, evidence of the waterfowlers' fine art. From scaup to goldeneyes to ruddy ducks and mergansers, from snow geese to Canada geese, a world of faux waterfowl is here for the viewing. The museum also acts as an agent for keeping local history and traditions alive; weekend programs include everything from decoy-carving workshops to clinics on "Down East–style" cooking.

Core Sound Waterfowl Museum is located at 1785 Island Road on Harkers Island. The museum's telephone number is (252) 728–1500. Hours are Monday through Saturday, 10:00 A.M. to 5:00 P.M., and Sunday from 2:00 to 5:00 P.M. The museum's Web site, www.coresound .com, has more information.

Mystery Ship
Hatteras Village

Of the hundreds of ships that have come to grief on the shoals and rough seas off the Outer Banks, none has done it more mysteriously than the *Carroll A. Deering*.

Launched in Bath, Maine, in 1919, the impressive five-masted schooner was on a return voyage from Rio de Janeiro, Brazil, in early 1921 when things went terribly wrong. At first light on the morning of January 31, a lookout at the Cape Hatteras Coast Guard station reported seeing a tremendous ship, with all sails set, wallowing on the Diamond Shoals, miles offshore.

Stormy seas meant it was days before Coast Guard ships could approach the *Deering* close enough to get a better look. When the sailors finally managed to climb on board, an eerie sight greeted them.

The ship's lifeboats were gone; rope ladders dangled limply down the ship's sides. Below decks the galley table was set as if the crew was just sitting down to a meal.

The *Deering*'s unexplained fate was front-page news around the country. Theories included abandonment at sea because of a mechanical failure, mutiny, attack by pirates, and a handful of other possibilities. But to this day no one actually knows what happened to the good ship and its sailors.

After a salvage crew scuttled her, remains from the formerly proud *Carroll A. Deering* washed ashore at Ocracoke Island. Later, the wreckage floated north and landed at Hatteras Island. In typical Outer Banks fashion, timbers from the ship became beams and joists for more than one islander's new home. A few of those timbers, a link of salt-chewed chain, and a rusty capstan are all—besides mystery—that remains of the "ghost ship of the Diamond Shoals."

Visit the Graveyard of the Atlantic Museum in Hatteras Village. The museum is located on a side road off Highway 12, just past the state ferry docks. For more information, call (252) 986–2995 or visit www.graveyardoftheatlantic.com.

The Carroll A. Deering sailed into mystery off the Carolina coast.

Bomb School
Hertford

Talk about your boomtowns. The quaint coastal community of Hertford (population around 2,000) in Perquimans County is home to farms, strings of small shops, marinas—and North Carolina's loudest secret.

The secret has an official name (the Harvey Point Defense Testing Activity) and an official proprietor (the Department of Defense). But don't let either of those details throw you off the scent. What Harvey Point really is, according to a slew of investigative news reports and memoirs by former intelligence officials, is the Central Intelligence Agency's main demolitions training facility. It's a place, you see, where all the boom-boom is quite hush-hush.

Big bangs: Here's where the CIA trains in demolitions.

The government has stuck to its cover story about Harvey Point for more than four decades. But by now it's something of an open secret that the high-security compound tucked into an otherwise quiet corner of marshland is the CIA's bomb school and has been since 1961.

For example, in his 2002 memoir, *See No Evil,* former CIA officer Robert Baer described the "two weeks of nonstop demolition training" he received at Harvey Point as a young spy recruit in the early 1970s: "We spent two days crimping blasting caps to make sure we understood that if you crimped them too high, they'd explode and take your hand off. After we'd mastered that, we crimped them in the dark, by feel. Then we started blowing things up: cars, buses, diesel generators, fences, bunkers. We made a school bus disappear with about 20 pounds of U.S. C-4 [plastic explosive]. . . . By the end of the training, we could have taught an advanced terrorism course."

In nearby Hertford, by now most people seem to be accustomed to all the boom and bang. "They're good neighbors," says a woman standing in the doorway of her home on Harvey Point Road who asks not to be identified. "They don't bother us and we don't bother them. It's for testing explosives, and that's all I know." The noise usually isn't a bother, she says, but "when they do one of the big ones, it jars everything, shakes everything for a few seconds."

Several times a month, the sound of the explosions is strong enough to carry 2 miles to the east, to Holiday Island. April Ghose grew up there.

"I heard it was FBI or CIA training, one of them," she says. "When I first moved down here, I didn't know what it was. My house started trembling, and I said, 'Grandma, what was that?' And she was like, 'It's just Harvey Point.' Now it's not a really big deal, I'm so used to it."

Anyone can look at overhead pictures of Harvey Point's blast-scarred grounds online—just do a search for "Harvey Point" and "CIA." But unless you've got a personal invitation from the government, take our advice—DO NOT try to visit in person.

How Great Thou Art

Holden Beach

Mary Paulsen spent nearly twenty years as a waitress in Calabash, a place famous for its delectable, fried seafood. Then she awoke one morning in 1996, and God commanded her to go into her garden and build a village to house the 6,000 dolls she had collected over the years. The work, He said, would help feed the hungry children of the world. Mary did as a true believer might and started building.

She built a train station, a candy-cane house, a soda shop, a library, a little red schoolhouse, and a Make-A-Wish-For-Jesus fountain. She filled her garden and festooned her trees with mobiles built from brightly painted steel cans and pots and pans.

In 1998 God commanded Paulsen to start painting on windows. As she explained to documentary filmmaker Blaire Johnson, "My husband and my mother-in-law [were] makin' fun of me, tellin' me I should do somethin' that was gonna turn into somethin' and I told them I was, and sure enough I had it sold before 10 o'clock the next mornin' at 80 dollars. That was my first one. They said my God, get her more windows. Help her. Get her paint and get her windows."

Paulsen's imaginative creations, her vivid artwork, and her infectious joy have turned her residence, now known as Mary's Gone Wild Folk Art and Doll Baby Museum, into a destination for lovers of "outsider art."

All of her artwork is fashioned from cast-off goods that otherwise would be destined for the landfill. Locals have taken to bringing likely supplies directly to her to feed what she calls her "gonna make you smile" art form.

"Everything that I do, like the windows that I recycle—all the tin cans and the glass jars and the wood pieces that I cut using pieces of scrap wood, all this," Paulsen told Johnson. "I say, 'Even if they throw it away later, it's going out of this county. It's not thrown away in this county. Brunswick County ought to be very happy! I've saved the landfill a bundle.'"

Paulsen's pint-size village is as charmed as it is unique. It has survived five hurricanes over the years, barely touched by winds that gusted in excess of 150 miles per hour. Of course Paulsen, a woman of faith, would probably tell you that something considerably bigger than good luck is at work here.

Mary's Gone Wild Folk Art and Doll Baby Museum is located at 2431 Holden Beach Road Southwest. To get there from Wilmington, take Highway 17 south for about 45 minutes until you reach Supply. After you pass the Supply Hospital, look for a sign on the left to Holden Beach. Turn left on Mt. Pisgah Road and travel 5.5 miles until you reach Holden Beach Road.

No Bones About It
Jamesville

There are very few places where you can still get a taste of river herring, which is a fate no one in eastern North Carolina would have predicted for the fish back in the day.

Returning each spring from the ocean to spawn, herring—a foot or so long and oily—used to teem in the state's eastern rivers. They took to the Tar, Pamlico, Roanoke, Chowan, and Pasquotank Rivers in numbers so dense that one could entertain the notion of walking bank to bank on them. In this hardscrabble part of the state, herring—dry-salted and cured or pickled—was the staple that kept the wolf from the door for many sharecropping families. Even fairly recently, you could buy herring for as little as a dollar a bucket from local fish houses.

Unfortunately, herring haven't taken as well to us as we did to them. Damming of rivers, overfishing, and pollution have all taken their toll on the fish. They still migrate up the big coastal rivers, but not in anything like the numbers they once did.

But if you're determined to try this ephemeral spring treat, probably no place is better equipped to satisfy your hankering than the Cypress Grill, an old plank-sided restaurant along the Roanoke River at Jamesville. For nigh seventy years the restaurant has served up mounds of herring during the fish's annual runs. If you can get around their fishy taste, the price is right: A plate of herring, french fries, coleslaw, and hush puppies costs a little more than $5.00.

Along with their considerable flavor, herring are famously bony, but the expert cooks at Cypress Grill take care of that. If you fry a herring long enough, the tiny bones more or less melt away.

Beginning about mid-January and running through late April, the Cypress Grill is open from 11:00 A.M. to 2:00 P.M. and 5:00 to 8:00 P.M. For directions, call (252) 792–4175.

Heavy Metal
Kill Devil Hills

There's a lot to see at the Museum of Printing; the trouble is actually getting to it. Located in a one-story brick building along the bypass that sends traffic to and from Outer Banks destinations, the museum has for years housed all of the devices and supplies once used in letterpress printing. Today, however, the place, which is a sort of annex to a used bookstore called the Croatoan Bookery Ltd., has a sleepy, defunct feeling.

The museum's centerpiece is a nineteenth-century Babcock Optimus Cylinder Press once used to print *The Roanoke News;* it ran nearly a century in that capacity. Other printing machines on display include the diminutive Chandler mini-press (cute!).

A breathtaking collection of metal type is on hand. Their messages, shown in reverse, are cryptic: BLOOD NEEDED. SUPPORT THE UNION MISSION. STREET CONDITIONS. ELLIS, TAXIDERMY. Also on display are the lead "slugs" that were melted down to produce the type.

The problem is that all of this fascinating stuff is cordoned off and turned in on itself, with piles of inexplicable goods piled nearby: ships' wheels, wooden trunks, a dusky lobster pot, among other items. The jumble is a testament to the collecting habits of the museum's owner, Francis Meekins, publisher of the Outer Banks's oldest family-run newspaper, *The Coastland Times*. For now the museum seems to be moribund, waiting for the touch of a dedicated curator to restore it to life.

The Museum of Printing is located at 2006 South Croatan Highway in Kill Devil Hills. Call (252) 480–1890 for hours and information about access.

Flight Control
Kitty Hawk

Even today, there are those hardcore doubters who believe that man has never been to the moon—that the much-publicized landings and moonwalks were staged by the government at some clandestine movie set.

Little wonder, then, that at the birthplace of flight there are still those who argue—stridently, if facetiously—that humans have never even left the ground, at least not in aircraft. The Man Will Never Fly Memorial Society carries as its motto "Birds Fly, Men Drink." In other words, rejecting the notion of air flight is their excuse for tossing a few back, and it makes for a good one.

On December 17, 1903, or so history records, Orville and Wilbur Wright lofted the first airplane on the sand dunes at Kitty Hawk. Gathering to take note of the accomplishment on December 16, 1959, a group of locals decided to say, "No way, no how." In jest but in earnest, they set out to smash the "myth" that the Wright brothers had taken to the skies, and to get smashed along the way. A society of the flightless was born.

Members "are not opposed to flight," notes the society's Web site, adding that, to borrow a line from Cole Porter, "Birds do it, bees do it, even educated fleas do it." But "we do not believe in flying machines," the site continues. "When you stop to think about it, do you actually believe that a machine made of tons of metal will fly? . . . We ask that you gather under our banner and combat the myth that man can, did, or will ever fly, except in his or her imagination."

True to its motto, the society—whose numbers nationwide are purported to be somewhere around 5,000—convenes in Kitty Hawk every December 16 to drink and debunk. The organization "has fought the hallucination of airplane flight with every weapon at its command, save sobriety," it proclaims. "We remain dedicated to the principle that two Wrights made a wrong at Kitty Hawk."

These people are only kidding . . . we think. To find out for yourself, or to join this well-lubricated bunch of aeronautical naysayers, visit www.manwillneverfly.com.

Maco Light
Maco

Poor Joe. He was only trying to do the right thing.

Way back in 1867, the dutiful conductor (last name Baldwin) was on board an Atlantic Coast Line train headed toward Wilmington when the car he was on seemed to be going nowhere.

Turns out that it had come uncoupled from the train before it and had come to a stop on the steel tracks. Seeing the lights of a following train growing closer, ol' Joe started waving his lantern back and forth frantically, trying to alert the train's conductor and head off a disaster.

Too bad, so sad: Joe perished when his car was smashed to bits by the locomotive bearing up behind it. His head was severed, but his lantern (so they say) still shines.

The so-called "Maco light" has been a supernatural fixture here since Joe's untimely death. In 1889 no less than an American president—Grover Cleveland—attested to seeing it.

The tracks at Maco were torn up in the 1970s, but you may still have a mind to go see what's left of the spectral Joe Baldwin. Be our guest.

Maco is located in Brunswick County, 12 miles northwest of Wilmington on U.S. Highway 74/76. The former site of the railroad crossing where Joe met his maker is located outside of town.

Grape Expectations
Manteo

Some people's front yards have a fine weeping cherry tree, or prized rose shrubs, or a nice shade oak. In their yard Jack and Estelle Wilson have what might be North America's most famous grapevine.

The Mother Vine is big—it erupts from Roanoke Island's sandy soil in a fat coil of stems as big around as a steel drum and throws its tangled shade over about 300 square feet of the Wilsons' yard. The Mother Vine is old, too, but there's no consensus on exactly how old. Depending on whom you ask, the vine is more than 500 years old, about 200 years old, or somewhat younger. Romantics and tourism hucksters are fond of saying that the vine was growing here when the first English settlers arrived in the late sixteenth century. Others are certain that settlers from the "lost colony" planted it as a hopeful act during their brief and tumultuous stay here. Still others pin the date as sometime in the eighteenth century, or possibly the nineteenth century.

Grapevines are rampant on Roanoke Island and, for that matter, in most of eastern North Carolina. In his 1584 chronicle, *First Voyage to Virginia,* English adventurer Arthur Barlowe described approaching the Outer

This sign in Manteo tells visitors they've missed the Mother Vine.

Banks and finding it a land "so full of grapes, as the very beating and surge of the Sea overflowed them."

The Mother Vine bears a bubblegum-sweet variety of muscadine grape called the Scuppernong, whose fruits have bronzy skins. The grape gets its name from a river that meanders through Tyrrell County, about 25 miles west of Roanoke Island on the mainland.

The vine used to be bigger; during the 1940s it covered more than an acre and furnished grapes for a local winery. If you ask around Roanoke Island, you might find someone who still has a bottle of the stuff.

Over the years Jack Wilson, who is retired from his many years as Manteo's fire chief, has taken a low-impact approach to his storied vine. He's trimmed it a little when it could use it. He's repaired the trellis here and there. Occasionally, he's given the vine a dose of oyster shells around the base for the lime they provide.

However old you fancy it, the vine is certainly impressive. And it just keeps growing, some years producing a bounty of sweet grapes. Its persistence across the centuries led native son William C. Etheridge to leave this poetic rumination about the "mother of all vines": "If once, while looking at the great twisted trunks, you happen to hear the drums and wild harp strings of a brawling sou'wester, you may wonder whether the old vine is under bond to grow grapes for the wine-press of the immortals."

The Mother Vine is located on private property along a bend of Mother Vineyard Road, 1.6 miles north of Manteo, a right-hand turn off northbound Business Highway 64.

She's an Egghead

Morehead City

No yolk—Marie Lawrence is quite serious about her collection of deviled-egg plates.

How serious? Well, as serious as you'd have to be to amass a collection of some 400 egg plates—and devote a wing of your house to displaying them. As if that weren't enough, her license plate reads EGGPLATE.

The egg-static collector caught the bug about ten years ago, and since then she's built a reputation as the nation's preeminent egg plate archivist. "The collection just snowballed," she explained to a reporter in 2006. "Each one is prettier than the last one, and I've never seen an ugly one."

So the next time you're scooping a deviled egg into your mouth—be it at a picnic or a potluck or in the privacy of your own home—think of Lawrence (and think about sending her your plate).

Here's to the Chrome Dome

Morehead City

If you think "bald is beautiful," you are not alone. If that's your credo or your bumper sticker, pack up the skull wax and head to Morehead City the second weekend in September. That's when the Bald-Headed Men of America (BHMA), headquartered there since its founding in 1973 by the resplendently bald John T. Capps III, holds its annual conference.

Touted as "the world's only organization that grows because of lack of growth," the BHMA stresses the fact that "our name may say 'men,' but our membership is open to all men, women and children around the world who believe 'bald is beautiful.'" And even if you can't make it to the conference, you can become a member, with numerous bald benefits—a subscription to the *Chrome Dome Bulletin,* a membership card, a copy of the group's official poem, and so on—for a mere $10. Bald is not only beautiful, but also cheap (think of the money saved on haircuts!).

For all the hairless details, check out the BHMA online at www .members.aol.com/baldusa, call (252) 726–1855, or e-mail jcapps 4102@aol.com.

Gifts from the Sea

Nags Head

Day in, day out, in calm weather or gale, Nellie Myrtle Pridgen walked her home stretch of beach at Nags Head, gathering what the sea brought her. Pridgen, who died in 1992, was by reputation a prickly, irascible woman, drawn more to nature than to her fellow man. She hated the course modern development was taking on the Outer Banks, and loved the changeable sands here far better than anything else. But Pridgen's personal quirks, and the single-mindedness of her lonely search, are our great fortune to share in.

Today, Pridgen's daughter, Carmen Gray, runs the small museum filled with her mother's findings. The collection is housed in the same place Pridgen assembled it—the old Mattie Midgette Store, a dusky, shingle-clad building along the Beach Road, in sight of Jockey's Ridge.

Inside are whelks, sharks' teeth, antique oil lamps, glass floats from Japanese fishing nets, and piles of colorful fishing lures. In one corner a worn hiking boot sprouts tendrils of orange coral, a sort of seaborne flower arrangement. Also on display is sea glass by the pound, sorted into its various colors. More delicate items, including paper-thin shells in all the colors of the spectrum, are kept in plastic boxes that once held leather wallets—prizes doled out at The Casino, another Nags Head landmark that's now gone.

Behind one glass case is the ornate spout from a seventeenth-century demijohn, bearing a fanciful, bearded face. An identical one was recovered from the 1626 wreck of the *Batavia,* off Australia's Great Barrier Reef. How this one made its way to the sands of Nags Head is anyone's guess. Another case contains a fulgurite—a blob of rock formed when a bolt of lightning struck the sand nearby.

But beyond the fulgurites, nautilus shells, and other wonders on display, the real charm of the museum lies in the plainness of much of it: the pails full of dried starfish, the piles of wormy wood, the Chianti bottles speaking of happy seamen. That is the power of the sea and sand, to take the most common objects and, by immersion and rough contact, elevate them to the sublime. Displayed here, baskets over-filled with lost toys—trucks without wheels, model soldiers with their features buffed away by the tides—somehow seem revelatory.

"I just think it's so sad that all of this is going away," says Gray, speaking of the traditional character of the Outer Banks. "And that's why I'm trying to preserve this little corner. It helps that people are so interested in it."

The Nellie Myrtle Pridgen Museum is located at 4008 South Virginia Dare Trail (the "beach road") in Nags Head, across from the historic cottage row district. It's adjacent to Jockey's Ridge, milepost 13. Call (252) 441–6259 for more information.

All Ashore That's Going Ashore
Nags Head

Some people have hobbies; other people have obsessions. Dr. Sarah Forbes's romance with the former cruise liner SS *United States* probably falls into the latter category.

The Virginia gynecologist grew up no stranger to big ships, sur-rounded, as she was, by the shipbuilding traditions of Norfolk and New-port News. But one ship in particular struck her fancy. The SS *United States* got the champagne treatment in 1952 and set off on a maiden voyage to Europe. The ship was three city-blocks long and capable of speeds of nearly 45 miles per hour and, moreover, had frills to burn.

In its day the *United States* carried the likes of John Wayne, Cary Grant, and Jackie Kennedy, not to mention royalty and international heads of state. After more than 400 ocean crossings, however, the cruise liner was retired due to the expense of operation and a general decline in passenger sea travel. At its saddest moment, the ship sat rusting along the Philadelphia, Pennsylvania, waterfront.

Forbes got wind of the ship's sale and purchased thousands of dollars' worth of memorabilia, fixtures, and trim from the luxe liner before it was gutted. They now adorn her Windmill Point Restaurant in Nags Head. We can't vouch for the food, never having eaten there, but you'd be hard-pressed to find a more curious interior in which to dine. An upstairs room has the *United States's* original kidney-shaped bar. Who better to tipple with than the ghosts of celebrities and ambassadors past?

The restaurant takes its name from the replica Outer Banks windmill that sits in the backyard, along Roanoke Sound, no small point of interest itself.

Windmill Point Restaurant and SS *United States* Lounge is located along U.S. Highway 158 in Nags Head, at milepost 16.5. Call (252) 441–1535 for permission to board.

Fred's Dead, But You Can See His Head

New Bern

Say the words "firehouse animal," and most folks immediately think of those trusty Dalmatians. But in New Bern, the first town in North Carolina to charter a fire company, it was a four-hoofed fellow who became the fireman's best friend.

His name was Fred. From 1908 to 1925 he pulled a New Bern Fire Department water wagon with dedication, speed, and bravery to match his human colleagues. Even as motorized trucks threatened to make him obsolete, he helped combat New Bern's worst fire ever—a 1922 conflagration that consumed more than 1,000 buildings. Three years later, he met his end on the job, collapsing as he shuttled a group of firefighters to what turned out to be a false alarm.

Fred's head is lovingly enshrined in a glass case at the Firemen's Museum at 408 Hancock Street. Dutiful as ever, he still wears his bridle. The museum, which also features vintage steam pumpers and other old-time firefighting gear, is open Monday through Saturday from 10:00 A.M. to 4:00 P.M. Admission is $5.00 for adults and $2.50 for children (kids under six get in free). For more information call (252) 636–4087 or visit www.newbern museums.com.

Fred forever: A fire horse's work is never done.

NOT A TAN LINE AMONG THEM

When you hit North Carolina's beaches, chances are you scale your wardrobe down to shorts, T-shirts, bathing suits, and the like. That's all well and good—but why stop there? The Outer Banks Nudist Club bares it all.

If you're reading this book cover to cover, this is the third nudist group you've come across. Rest assured that this will be the last; and know that, as with the other two, we'll refrain from the temptation to make them the butt of jokes.

The club has periodic, carefully planned get-togethers on (usually) remote beaches. Along the way it has learned to operate without ruffling too many feathers among those who aren't accustomed to the unclothed. Rules and suggestions posted on the outfit's official Web site (www.obxnudistclub.com) include the following:

- "Because of the nature of beaches on the Outer Banks and the isolation needs of a naturist/nudist club, the best beaches are beaches that can only be reached by boat. Because most of these areas are controlled by the Park Service, which, while not approving of naturist/nudist activities, seems to be taking a hands-off attitude, caution is strongly urged. Please do not

sunbathe in areas frequented by the more inhibited tourists."
(That would be most areas.)

- "Please, please pick up after yourself. Nothing will draw more unwanted attention from the Park Service than leaving trash behind." (Well, maybe nothing more than dozens of naked people.)

- "Guys, if you are single, please try to get a date before you arrive at a get-together. Nudist clubs are not a good place to find single women, and you will be asked to leave if you hit on members." (For whatever reason, there's no similar admonition against women showing up seeking men.)

- "Taking pictures without . . . permission is not allowed under any circumstances." (But permissions are sometimes given, as evidenced by the club's photo page on the Internet. *Full* disclosure: The page offers full disclosure.)

So if you're strolling the North Carolina sands and suddenly come across a group wearing birthday suits, remember that they're probably trying to play by the rules (and that you can always look away).

Where They Buried the Brits

Ocracoke Island

In early 1941 German U-boats marauded the North Carolina coast, sinking merchant vessels in numbers averaging one a day. Outer Banks residents could watch the greatest of sea dramas playing out off their beaches: tankers and cargo ships, stricken, burning, sinking just a few miles from shore.

The U.S. military, taken off guard by Pearl Harbor, wasn't yet in fighting mode and was unable to ward off the U-boat threat. In the absence of domestic help, twenty-four ships from Britain's Royal Navy were sent to assist with patrol and escort duties along the mid-Atlantic coast. The ungainly fleet, consisting of converted fishing trawlers, was known as "Harry Tate's Navy," after an English entertainer of the time.

One of the ships was HMS *Bedfordshire*. On the night of May 11, 1942, the hunter became the hunted when the *Bedfordshire* entered the sights of the German submarine *U-558*. A torpedo sent the British vessel to the bottom, with the loss of everyone on board.

A few days after the ship sank, four bodies washed up on Ocracoke Island.

The men—only two of whom could be identified—were buried in a small fenced graveyard on the island, which is maintained today by the British War Graves Commission.

Each morning a Union Jack is raised over the cemetery by members of the U.S. Coast Guard, and a special ceremony, remembering those who died, is held each May.

The men are memorialized in a plaque inscribed with the words of Robert Brooke: "If I should die, think only this of me—that there's some forever corner of a foreign field that is forever England."

Ocracoke is a small place and best explored on foot. Nearly anyone will be willing—and capable—of telling you where the British Cemetery is located.

Christmas Again?

Rodanthe

O Christmas, must you come only once a year? Not in Hatteras Island's Rodanthe, where locals are willing to give the holiday a whirl in both December and January.

And no, it's not some marketing gimmick, some post-holiday excuse to mark down and move a few consumer goods. Instead, it's a nod to a long, if murky, local history.

It appears that "Old Christmas," which Rodanthe has celebrated in early January for more than a century, is a relic of the colonial era. In 1752 the British empire switched to the Georgian calendar, which was eleven days shorter than the going rate. In the American colonies not everyone got the word—and when they got it in Rodanthe, they pretty much ignored it, celebrating Christmas on their own schedule. Eventually, the town came to mark the holiday twice.

The Old Christmas celebration is still held at the Rodanthe Community Center on the Saturday closest to Epiphany. It starts with an afternoon oyster roast, and after everyone chows down, it's time for Old Buck—a stuffed rendition of a mythical wild bull that is said to have traumatized the town long ago—to take center stage.

Sound strange? Maybe so—but perhaps no stranger than a red-suited fat man who travels by reindeer sled and slides down your chimney to eat cookies and drop off presents. The occasion is a decidedly local affair, but visitors can find some details at the Outer Banks Chamber of Commerce Web site at www.outer-banks.com.

The Root of It All

Sneads Ferry

You can't blame a man for getting sentimental about his soda pop, especially if he feels a personal attachment to it. So it goes with Jerome Gundrum, who is quite possibly the biggest root beer devotee in the world.

Wait a minute, you might say: Lots of folks like the carbonated confection, so how could any one of them stake a claim to being root beer's number one fan? Well, Gundrum can prove it—as a quick visit to his Dr. Rootbeer's Hall of Foam will attest. The old-fashioned soda shop in Sneads Ferry is pretty much the first and last word in root beer.

Thirsty for proof? Just try one of his root beer floats as you peruse items from his collection of 4,000 root beer–related relics, which he has poured his heart and soul into since he picked up a DAD's root beer sign in 1974. Today, he has amassed some 600 vintage company signs, including a Hires variety dating from the late 1890s, the earliest in the collection. Then there are the bottles, the mugs, the souvenirs of every size and shape.

And Gundrum doesn't just guzzle the stuff; he brews it too. Stop by the place to have a taste. The Hall of Foam is located at 288 Fulcher's Landing Road; call (910) 327–ROOT for hours and directions. If you can't make it there, at least sample the history and pictures featured at the store's delicious Web site (www.rootbeer.net).

Homer Simpson Doesn't Work Here

Southport

Hmm, how can we put this? Let's just say that opinions about the propriety of nuclear power, well, differ. But that's an issue for another book; in this one, it's our sworn duty to inform you of a chance to visit one of the country's rare nuclear power public attractions.

You read that right. We're talking about the Progress Energy Brunswick Plant Visitors Center, where you can get up close and personal with an energy source that some folks would just prefer to keep some distance from. "Come explore the world of energy," a brochure invites. "Interactive exhibits, graphic displays and videos will enlighten and entertain people of all ages. You and your family will have a better understanding of nuclear power and other energy sources used in our world today." What's more, you can "use a Geiger counter to measure amounts of radioactivity in various objects"—and then retire for a snack in the center's picnic area.

The center, at 8520 River Road Southeast, is closed on weekends and holidays, and hours vary on weekdays. Call (910) 457–2418 for directions and up-to-date information. Admission is free (as are state Department of Transportation maps to "evacuation shelters," should something go awry).

Nuclear power, up close and personal.

Rockets in Their Pocket

Topsail Beach

As top-secret code names go, Operation Bumblebee doesn't sound so serious. But don't be fooled: The operation helped build long-range missiles that could leave quite a sting, so to speak.

Today, there's no better place to learn about Bumblebee than the Topsail Island Museum, which carries the slogan "Missiles and More." True, the museum has more than just missiles. But there's no denying that the prototype weapons are the pointy heart of the museum, which is located inside the building where the projectiles were assembled.

Bumblebee had a short but influential flight. The operation, which ran from 1946 to 1948, proved essential in the development of the two-stage ramjet engine—the kind used for supersonic flight. Along the way some 200 experimental missiles were fired from Topsail into the sea, with the farthest ones flying 40 miles out.

Don't worry: These missiles are all duds.

The museum opened in 1997 and was expanded considerably in 2005. It features missile specimens (including one that washed up on the beach in 1994), a video of Bumblebee test launches, and an interactive media center describing Camp Davis, a local military outpost. It also hosts regular special presentations on topics ranging from "Memories of the Bumblebee Project" to "Women Air Force Service Pilots—WASP at Camp Davis."

And if missiles aren't your thing, there's plenty more to see, including exhibits on the area's natural history, historic pirates, and local Native Americans.

The Topsail Island Museum, at 720 Channel Boulevard, is open April through mid-October from 2:00 to 4:00 P.M. on Monday, Tuesday, Thursday, Friday, and Saturday. From November to March, visits and group tours can be arranged. For details, directions, and arrangements, call (800) 626–2780 or visit www.topsailmuseum.org.

Hover Near

Weeksville

Ever wonder where blimps go during "downtime"? A visit to the gigantic, cavernous blimp hangars at Weeksville will deflate that question considerably.

Blimps, airships, dirigibles: Whatever you call them, they've been floating overhead and hovering in the news at least since the 1930s, when the hydrogen-filled German airship *Hindenburg* went up in flames. Here in Weeksville the bloated craft have made a home since the 1940s.

Answering the threat of German U-boats during the first months of World War II, the U.S. Navy moved its eastern airship operations to Weeksville Naval Air Station in June 1942. The compound, on the outskirts of Elizabeth City, spanned nearly 1,000 acres and had a steel

Nothing quite says "national defense" like an enormous bag of gas.

hangar big enough to accommodate twelve Navy "K" airships, with room besides for 700 enlisted men and 150 officers. A second hangar, built of wood and 1,028 feet long, was finished in 1943.

The blimp world was a golden place until the 1950s, when the helicopter superseded the plodding airships.

Nevertheless, the Weeksville facility managed to get a stay of execution in 1971, when blimp manufacturer TCOM L.P. and Westinghouse Airships Inc. moved in, crafting airships for the commercial trade. The wooden hangar burned in 1995, but the company rallied and has centered operations in the 300,000-square-foot steel hangar ever since. For tours of the impressive facility, call (252) 330–5555.

Another company, Airship Management Services (AMS), rents space at the Weeksville site and, from time to time, offers blimp rides. Call AMS in Elizabeth City at (252) 330–3010 to find out more.

Sssssssstay a While

Wilmington

Dean Ripa has been bitten by venomous snakes ten times. Remarkably, in addition to still being alive, Ripa still likes snakes.

He has collected them since childhood. To make a living, he once traveled around the world, brought rare snakes back to Wilmington, and bred them for sale to zoos and institutes. When his collection of fanged reptiles got too big, he started a zoo of his own to put them on display.

The Cape Fear Serpentarium is probably the world's most well-appointed collection of deadly snakes. There are enough rattlers and asps and pit vipers to make your head spin (and your heart skip a beat). They are displayed in a naturalistic setting, with palms and rubber trees, sand, and cacti in place to make the snakes feel like they never left home. If snakes simply aren't enough, there are crocodiles and a dragon-sized monitor lizard to restore your curiosity.

If you're not a snake lover like Ripa, you may be forgiven. Humans have had an abiding fear of ol' mister no-neck since at least the days of Adam and Eve. But if you're keen to learn more about (and long to be closer to) these most misunderstood of creatures, you won't do better than a visit to the Cape Fear Serpentarium. It's located on Orange Street, between River and Front Streets, along the Cape Fear River waterfront in downtown Wilmington. Hours are 11:00 A.M. to 5:00 P.M. on weekdays and 11:00 A.M. to 6:00 P.M. Saturday and Sunday. Call (910) 762–1669 or visit www.capefearserpentarium.com for more information.

A Man's Best Friend, Forever

Wilmington

It gets lonely on a riverboat, if you don't have a friend nearby. Same goes for the grave, where most of us will pass the time alone.

William Ellerbook is one man who never had to worry about either problem: He spent his days on earth with his best dog buddy, Boss. And unlike most dog owners, he'll spend his remaining days *under* the earth with his pup.

In February 1870 Ellerbrook and Boss were devoured by a fire on the waterfront. The story goes that Boss went down trying to rescue his master.

Whether or not that's true, the two beings will slumber together from here on out. They're buried in a plot together at Oakdale Cemetery, where a grave marker sponsored by local firefighters offers one of the most poignant pet-cemetery moments you'll find on this planet. On the backside of the stone is a relief carving of Boss, ever watchful over Ellerbrook. The inscription reads "Faithful Until Death."

The cemetery is located at 530 North 15th Street in Wilmington.

Can Your Zoo Do That?

Wilmington

The animal park that formerly billed itself as the "Tote-Em-Inn Zoo" has operated at this resort city in some fashion for more than fifty years, long enough to become a tourist staple. And yes, the namesake animals at Tregembo Animal Park are plenty interesting (there are nearly one hundred species of them, including giraffe, lion, tiger, zebra, bear, and monkeys). Nevertheless, it's all the other stuff that really sets this place apart.

To wit: a "Worldwide Oddity Museum" that contains hundreds of items you'd be unlikely to spy anywhere else. Wooden seats that were once used by President and Mrs. Ronald Reagan on a visit to Wilmington. A collection of ceremonial masks from around the world. A sacred Indonesian figure, roughly life-size. Nearly one hundred relics of primitive man. A "War Room" depicting military history through the centuries. A collection of swords, spears, axes, and other dire metal implements, spanning the walls. An exhibit featuring news headlines about some of the world's more notable circus freaks. This is not your ordinary zoo, friend.

And, lest you overlook it, there is a whole separate building devoted to the art and science of taxidermy in all its stitched and stuffed glory, including quite a few creatures lying on shelves nearby, pickled in institutional-size jars of formaldehyde. The animal park also has a 4,000-square-foot gift store. Miss all of this only at your great loss.

The park is open Friday through Sunday only. To get there, follow U.S. Highway 421 South to 5811 Carolina Beach Road. Call (910) 392–3604 or visit www.tregemboanimalpark.com for current admission prices.

Enter at your own risk at Tregembo Animal Park.

INDEX

INDEX

INDEX

INDEX

INDEX

INDEX

About the Authors

Kent Priestley and Jon Elliston are writers and editors for Asheville, North Carolina's independent newsweekly, the *Mountain Xpress*. Their writing on history, politics, culture, food, and other sundry topics has appeared in publications from coast to coast.

They hope to remain friends.